ONE

WRITER'S

REALITY

ONE
WRITER'S
REALITY

~

Monroe K. Spears

UNIVERSITY OF MISSOURI PRESS
Columbia and London

Copyright © 1996 by
The Curators of the University of Missouri
University of Missouri Press, Columbia, Missouri 65201
Printed and bound in the United States of America
All rights reserved
5 4 3 2 1   00 99 98 97 96

Library of Congress Cataloging-in-Publication Data

Spears, Monroe Kirklyndorf.
    One writer's reality / Monroe K. Spears.
       p.   cm.
    Includes index.
    ISBN 0-8262-1049-X (cloth : alk paper)
    1. American literature—History and criticism.   2. English poetry—History and criti-
cism.   3. Authorship.   I. Title.
    PS121.S548   1996
    810.9—dc20   95-43008
                                                                                      CIP

∞ ™ This paper meets the requirements of the
American National Standard for Permanence of Paper
for Printed Library Materials, Z39.48, 1984.

Designer: Kristie Lee
Typesetter: BOOKCOMP
Printer and binder: Thomson-Shore, Inc.
Typeface: Berkeley

To my dear wife

Betty, without whom

neither I nor this little book

would now exist

CONTENTS

I HOPE MY TITLE doesn't mislead anyone into thinking this is a formal treatise on metaphysics or critical theory. It contains, in fact, no rigorous or fully developed argument. A broad and varied suggestiveness seemed to me a more appropriate method of presenting my remarkably simple basic thesis that the writer is not essentially different from the reader and of distinguishing the kinds of reality writers have to confront and deal with. Since this book is designed to be short, informal, and personal, I have eliminated all but minimal references. Some of these pieces were addressed to a specific audience, such as the presumably serious writers who attend writers' conferences, as well as to the general reader. When the places and occasions are significant, they are mentioned in a footnote.

The chapters are arranged so as to consider reality from the largest scale in "Cosmology" to the smallest and most personal scale in the last one. "Writing as a Vocation" is a kind of introduction. It concludes that economic reality is (fortunately) unimportant to the writer; what must in the end matter to him, as to the reader, are the deeper realities of place and community, human relations and emotions, and aesthetic form, and ultimately the transmutation of daily life into the ideal reality of form in art. The next two chapters discuss the specific historical example of Sewanee, the *Sewanee Review* at its centennial, and related matters. Then there are two examples of reality as seen by two very different poets, Dickey and Auden. One novelist, Reynolds Price, is discussed, with particular reference to his dealings with passion and the supernatural. Next comes a somewhat venturesome and speculative essay on the expression of emotion in music and poetry, comparing Schubert and Keats, especially as they confronted the final reality of death. The last chapter is very personal and specific, about some of the realities of my own life.

I would like to thank Wyatt Prunty, Director of the Sewanee Writers' Conference, for suggesting and commissioning several of these pieces, and the editors of the periodicals in which some of them have appeared: Frederick Morgan and Paula Deitz of *Hudson Review*, Dave Smith of *Southern Review*, George Core of *Sewanee Review*, and Mark Winchell of *South Carolina Review*.

ACKNOWLEDGMENTS

THE FOLLOWING pieces are reprinted by permission:

"Cosmology and the Writer," *Hudson Review* 47 (1994), 29–45. Copyright (c) 1994 by Monroe K. Spears.

"James Dickey's Poetry," *Southern Review* 30 (1994), 751–60. Copyright (c) by Louisiana State University; assigned to Monroe K. Spears June 24, 1995.

"The *Sewanee Review* and the Southern Renascence," *South Carolina Review* 25 (1992), 7–11. Copyright (c) 1992 by Clemson University.

"On Being Inducted into the South Carolina Academy of Authors," *South Carolina Review* 26 (1993), 181–86. Copyright (c) 1993 by Clemson University.

"Reflections on the Centennial of the *Sewanee Review*," *Sewanee Review* 100 (1992), 657–61. Copyright (c) 1992 by Monroe K. Spears.

"Auden Twenty Years After," *Sewanee Review* 102 (1994), 476–82. Copyright (c) 1994 by Monroe K. Spears.

"Scenes from a Marriage," *Washington Post Book World,* April 10, 1988. Copyright (c) 1988 by the Washington Post Book World Service/Washington Post Writers Group.

"The Mystery of Particular Spaces," *Raleigh News and Observer,* June 27, 1993. Copyright (c) 1993 by the *Raleigh News and Observer.*

ONE

WRITER'S

REALITY

CHAPTER 1

~

Writing

as a

Vocation

IS WRITING REALLY a vocation, "a simple calling like any other," as some critics have described it? If it is a vocation at all, it is certainly not simple. To begin with, it does not provide a livelihood, or not one you can count on; the one thing no serious writer—no rhapsode, bard, scop, minstrel, troubadour, court poet, or modern playwright, poet, or novelist—has ever said about his occupation is, "Well, it's a living." Journalism, writing scripts for TV and movies, and producing genre fiction—detective, mystery, police procedural, spy, romance, horror, technothriller, science, suspense, children's or teenagers'—may provide a reliable and sometimes handsome income; but, as Katherine Anne Porter memorably put it, "there are other and surer and much more honest ways of making money, and Mama advises you to look about and investigate them before leaping into such a gamble as mercenary authorship."[1] Nor has writing ever, in the United States, provided the writer a recognized place in the community. It is certainly not a profession like law or medicine, with its own self-policing standards and an accepted fiduciary relationship with clients.[2] The "man of letters" has

1. *Collected Essays and Occasional Writings* (New York: Delacorte Press, 1970), 461.
2. John Gross, *The Rise and Fall of the Man of Letters: A Study of the Idiosyncratic and the Humane in Modern Literature* (New York: Macmillan, 1969), 28.

a long history in France and England, but has existed in America largely as myth. Since World War II, with few exceptions, serious writers in this country have in fact been supported mainly by academia, and an enormous industry has developed known as Writing Programs, or Creative Writing, or, more jauntily, CW. In addition to the opportunists always ready to profit from the public's dreams of easy money ("How do you know you can't write? Make millions at home in your spare time!") many universities as well as correspondence schools are now all too ready to teach whatever students want, or think they want. But more is involved than mere cynical exploitation.

Why do so many people in this country want to write, or want to think of themselves as creative writers? I speak as one of them; but my attitude to such questions has certainly been influenced, and probably skewed, by my early experience as editor of a literary quarterly of high standards and low circulation. No one who has not had such experience can fully appreciate how many would-be poets and fiction writers there are, all clamoring for publication, few showing definite signs of talent. If there are still mute inglorious Miltons blushing unseen and wasting their sweetness on the desert air, any modern editor would have to say: most of them are inglorious, all right; but they are anything but mute. My attitude has also been affected by the increasing psychobabble over the years about "creativity," which assumes that everyone is creative and values equally all attempts at self-expression, from finger-painting and macramé to poetry. This background may have inclined me to make too rigid and absolute a distinction between the talented and the untalented, the serious and the popular or merely entertaining. At any rate, I feel that the time has come for me to reconsider such questions and try to resolve some of my own ambivalences. In addition to the general reader I always hope for, I have had in mind the particular audience of aspiring writers who have already demonstrated some talent and commitment to developing it; my intention is to offer them a realistic perspective of the literary vocation against a larger background.

The Romantic notion of the writer as superior being, not subject to the laws and limitations of ordinary humans, or as sacrificial victim redeeming the rest of mankind, no longer seems plausible to many people. Yet the serious writer's vocation obviously does have a spiritual dimension, which we must recognize, however we define it. The writer's true vocation—his ultimate aim and function—may be described broadly as the incorporation in form of his vision and perception of human life. His personal aims and motives—the desire for fame and money, for love, for sympathy and perhaps for complicity—may be urgent and fascinating but are subordinate to this basic function.

It is important to distinguish between the two meanings of vocation as everyday livelihood and as transcendent goal, but not possible to keep them wholly separate. Writers in the past have never been able to, and one of the major themes of poetry has been the poet's frustration in both at once—laments for his empty purse, complaints for his neglect by the public, by his cruel fair, his coy mistress, his recalcitrant Muse; palinodes in which he gives up the whole thing as a bad job. I want to follow both of these strands—the relation of the writer to the real world, or society as it is, and his relation to an ideal or spiritual world—though I cannot hope to keep them always disentangled.

Writing as a profession—that is, a profession that allows a "man of letters" to support himself comfortably and respectably by serious writing—is possible in the United States only for a very few very lucky individuals, mostly novelists or playwrights. Things are somewhat easier in France, Germany, or England, where the serious writer has proportionately larger audiences and where he can supplement his income by writing for weekly or monthly periodicals or appearing on state-supported radio and television. The writer is a respected and admired figure in Europe; in the United States he is likely to be regarded as frivolous or shiftless, foolishly trying to make a living through what should be a hobby or avocation. Faulkner was called by his neighbors "Count No-'count," and Ralph Ellison was thought by his Harlem neighbors to be in the numbers racket because he didn't go out to work.

A few statistics, however unreliable, may give some notion of the numbers involved: there were eighty-two thousand "authors" in the United States in 1989, according to *Statistical Abstracts;* up from sixty-two thousand in 1969. (Some directories list sixty-six hundred published poets and novelists in the United States; the others are presumably unpublished, or are not poets or novelists.) The Center for the Social Sciences at Columbia did a statistical survey in 1979 finding that 46 percent of American writers held other jobs, and one-fourth earned less than one thousand dollars annually; American writers averaged less than five thousand dollars a year. James L. W. West puts the plight of the American writer plainly: "In cold economic terms, authors have been common laborers."[3] There are, according to Joseph Epstein, only about two hundred American authors who support themselves primarily from their writing. This number would include, I suppose, the whole range from the few genuine writers at the top to writers like Danielle Steel and Jackie Collins at the bottom, who thrive on the public's fantasies of the private lives of the rich and famous. The bottom in literary merit is often the top in economic reward; recent examples are the enormous sums—$8 million for the TV rights alone—earned by Alexandra Ripley's *Scarlett* in spite of uniformly bad reviews, and the 157 weeks on the best-seller list, with forthcoming movie, of *The Bridges of Madison County,* by Robert James Waller, a professor of management who seems to write according to the precepts of that profession. (How would these two fit Henry James's definition of the artist as "the one individual who gives a permanent and enduring shape to a life that is evanescent and perishable"?) At the same time, as more and more magazines and publishing houses are taken over by consortiums interested only in profits, it becomes harder and harder for the serious novelist or poet to get published at all, and collections of serious stories or essays are even less marketable.

As to the place of the writer in society: the tendency is to assume, in the United States, that he doesn't have any, being either above or below it. The rise and fall of the man of letters in England was essentially a nineteenth-century phenomenon, according to John Gross. "Man of Letters" first meant scholar, learned man, then (gradually) professional author; by 1840 Carlyle can write of the Hero as Man of Letters. But the term soon began to take on the connotation of second-order writer—critic, teacher, or journalist, rather than poet, novelist, or playwright—and, though it could be used for the English Men of Letters series that began in the 1870s, it fell into disrepute, according to Gross, by 1914,

---

3. *American Authors and the Literary Marketplace Since 1900* (Philadelphia: University of Pennsylvania Press, 1988), 20.

and became almost extinct in England. But in the United States, as we shall see, the situation was quite different.

Let us now leave the discouraging topic of the dwindling financial prospects of the serious writer, and consider the more important rewards he may still look forward to. The conception of writers as constituting an ideal or mythical state goes far back in time; the OED cites "commonwealth of learning" and "commonwealth of letters" from the seventeenth century and "republic of letters" from Addison on, "commonwealth" suggesting a community of shared interests and "republic" "any community . . . in which there is a certain equality among the members." (Samuel Johnson speaks of the "great republic of humanity" and George Washington at Harvard of "your literary republic.") Randall Jarrell defines art as constituting an ideal order beyond time, and quotes "the greatest of the writers of this century, Marcel Proust" describing the death of his fictional writer, Bergotte:

> Everything is arranged in this life as though we entered it carrying the burden of obligations contracted in a former life; there is no reason inherent in the conditions of life on this earth that can make us consider ourselves obliged to do good, to be fastidious, to be polite even, nor make the talented artist consider himself obliged to begin over again a score of times a piece of work the admiration aroused by which will matter little to his body devoured by worms, like the patch of yellow wall painted with so much knowledge and skill by an artist who must forever remain unknown and is barely identified under the name Vermeer. All these obligations which have not their sanction in our present life seem to belong to a different world, founded upon kindness, scrupulosity, self-sacrifice, a world entirely different from this . . . [4]

Lewis Simpson has developed most fully the historical and religious implications of this conception. He quotes Auden who, in 1967, accepted an award "in the name of all my fellow-citizens in the Republic of Letters, that holy society which knows no national frontiers, possesses no military hardware, and where the only political duty on all of us at all times is to love the Word and defend it against its enemies." The

4. Randall Jarrell, *Poetry and the Age* (New York: Noonday Press, 1953), 26–27.

imagination of this catholic, sacramental community has been, Simpson says, a dominant motive in the twentieth-century American vocation to letters. He traces the conception back to the ideal cosmopolis of the Stoics (to which men belong because they participate in the Logos) and to Arcadia and the Virgilian vision of pastoral as an independent world. "The unfolding distinction of the realm of letters as a realm of being is enhanced . . . by the Christian ecumenicalism of the Word," with its concepts of the City of God and Republic of Christ. But Baudelaire's declaration, "The man of letters is the world's enemy," is the slogan of the great modern movement in literature: "Marked by the defection of the most original literary minds from society, this may be called the Great Literary Secession" and "governs the concept of the literary vocation which gives us the modern image of the man of letters as a prophet-priest-artist. At once a man of solitude and a member of a community, or an order, of literary alienation, he is a figure often absurd yet often heroic."[5]

The New Criticism, Simpson argues, was "a symbolic expression of the autonomy of the literary realm . . . to preserve the realm of letters as an order of society." Allen Tate summed it up in his 1952 address, "The Man of Letters in the Modern World": "It is the duty of the man of letters to supervise the culture of language to which the rest of culture is subordinate, and to warn us when our language is ceasing to forward the ends proper to man. The end of social man is communion in time through love, which is beyond time." But this address, Simpson says, "may possibly mark not only the terminal date of the New Criticism but of the whole modern movement toward the renewal of the literary order in America." The cause, he suggests, is the "displacement of the humanistic concept of the verbal center of civilization. . . . In our society in general the 'discipline' of letters is largely outmoded, and literary expression itself is becoming a marginal competitor for attention among the innovative modes of expression produced by technology. . . . The 'man of letters' has become obsolete." Simpson's pessimism here is, I hope and believe, excessive.

5. *The Man of Letters in New England and the South: Essays on the History of the Literary Vocation in America* (Baton Rouge: Louisiana State University Press, 1973), 229, 208–9.

France has always been the envy of both England and the United States in respect for literature: Matthew Arnold admired the society in which Joubert and Sainte-Beuve could flourish, and Irving Babbitt wrote reverently of the *Masters of Modern French Criticism* (1912). Richard Bernstein[6] describes how the present-day French buy and read more books proportionately, and support higher journalism, than any other nation. France offers more literary prizes per capita than any other country; more serious books (philosophy, history, politics) are published and sold, and there is more debate over them. The major book club, France Loisirs, sells twenty-six million books per year, or roughly one for every two people in France. "Apostrophes," the fifteen-year-old Friday night TV show, consisted of seventy-five minutes in which the host, Bernard Pivot, talked with a small group of writers; it regularly got 15 percent of TV viewers. Apparently the closest rivals of the French in avidity for books and respect for authors are the Russians and other formerly Communist nations, though throughout Europe the standard is much higher than in the United States. Japan, too, far surpasses the United States.

It is important to realize that subsidy of writers by teaching is, for the most part, restricted to the United States and is a quite recent development, on a large scale only since the Second World War. For the teaching writer, this is probably a very good thing; if he or she has some reputation, mobility and freedom can be kept with minimum financial anxiety. According to the *AWP* (Associated Writing Programs) *Chronicle,* AWP has grown from 13 programs in the 1960s to 201 now; the *Chronicle* is read by more than twelve thousand students, writers, and teachers. Its Catalogue has information on 328 graduate and undergraduate writing programs in the United States and Canada, classified as Studio, Studio/Academic, and Traditional with Concentration in Creative Writing. ("Studio" apparently means that the students' own writings are the only subject of study in the course or program.) Other sources say that in 1989 there were 250 writing programs in the United States alone, plus a large number of summer writing conferences. I have sometimes had a nightmare vision of AWP as a giant reciprocating

6. *Fragile Glory: A Portrait of France and the French* (New York: Knopf, 1990).

mechanism, a self-sufficient subculture in which self-professed writers become teachers of writing without ever establishing a reputation in the outside world, and students and teachers alone read each other, take in each other's washing, in an isolated self-contained community. AWP as acronym sounds dreadfully like Whitman's "barbaric yawp" writ large over the rooftops of the world. Yet obviously writing programs give aspiring authors time and stimulation, at the least, and assure the developing writer of a sympathetic and intensely interested audience. My attitude toward such programs has changed from initial skepticism to admiration for those that are well planned and administered and real enthusiasm for the summer Writers' Conference in which I have been participating since my return to Sewanee.

In sharp contrast, in England there are only two M.A. programs in writing, one established in the early 1970s at the University of East Anglia by Malcolm Bradbury and Angus Wilson and the other during the past decade at the University of Lancaster by David Craig. Each supports an average of six students per year. Over the past twenty years, one hundred students completed East Anglia's M.A. program, while there were one thousand applicants for 1990 alone. So these are far smaller and more elitist than American programs, though there have recently been signs of rapid growth.

Only in the United States is it possible for a writer to make a significant amount of money by giving readings and lectures to book clubs and academic audiences and to have all the privileges of academic tenure, and often more, simply for teaching the art and craft of writing. In our culture, the sad fact is that a poet can make much more money by talking or writing about his art than by practicing it. It is not that writers are more highly regarded here than in France, Germany, or England— in fact the reverse appears to be true—but that their audiences and students in this country seem to hope that the writers will impart to them some magic secret that will enable them to become writers too.

If writing can't be a vocation in the economic meaning, neither can it possibly be an avocation, spare-time amusement, hobby, in any sense except the economic: the writer will probably have to earn his living in some other way. Ideally, it would be both at once, as Robert Frost put it in "Two Tramps in Mud-Time":

My object in living is to unite
My avocation and my vocation
As my two eyes make one in sight.
Only where love and need are one,
And the work is play for mortal stakes,
Is the deed ever really done
For Heaven and the future's sakes.

But in an imperfect world, the element of play is rarely central. Writers write because they *need* to write, as an intimate part of their psychic makeup. In Meredith Skura's formulation: the writer (or creative person in general, including scientists) as infant loves the sensory world and is powerfully drawn to it; then some trauma (often the death of a parent) ends this love affair with the world, makes him withdraw from it, turn away; and his art, channeled through a particular medium (words, paint, clay, musical sound), is essentially an effort to recapture or re-create this lost world. What makes the artist different "is that his art is his world, and his work is his love life; it is an end in itself . . . for no other audience except the fantasied one in his own mind."[7] Art begins as therapy in this sense, she says, then becomes independent of the artist's conflicts.

Some analysts regard all psychotherapy as essentially writing (and vice versa): what the analyst and patient do is work out together a coherent and mutually satisfactory version of the patient's autobiography. Writing produced in this way (unless the analyst takes over as ghost writer) may be effective as psychotherapy, but is unlikely to be of much interest to the general public. There are, however, some examples to the contrary, most notably Lowell's *Life Studies*.

"Love's not so pure, and abstract, as they use / To say, which have no Mistresse but their Muse," said Donne in "Loves Growth." But perhaps no writer finally has any other; his complaints of his mistress's coyness become more and more transparently complaints of the Muse's refusal to come when invited. So the desire to write is a siren song as well as highest ambition, for the writer may at last have to give up human

---

7. "Creativity: Transgressing the Limits of Consciousness," *Daedalus* 109 (spring 1980 [Proceedings of the American Academy of Arts and Sciences]), 143.

love. If the Muse should call, we assume, who would not answer? But any psychological or vocational counselor would have to advise against picking up the phone.

In reaction against Romantic over-valuation, T. S. Eliot, W. H. Auden, and sometimes James Joyce (who once said he had the mind of a grocer's assistant) all suggest that the artist is essentially an ordinary man except for his talent, that there are no exemptions from any requirements, moral or economic, on account of "genius." But the artist is not "normal." Plato's view in the *Ion* and *Phaedrus* that poets are mad was extreme, but certainly not without evidence, from the ancient stories about the suicides of Empedocles and Lucretius to very numerous modern instances. "Great wits are sure to madness near allied, / And thin partitions do their bounds divide," as Dryden put it.

Writing may serve as a form of psychotherapy, as Robert Graves, Robert Lowell, and many followers of the "confessional" movement in poetry have demonstrated. Graves and Lowell both took up writing as therapy prescribed by their psychiatrists; Pat Conroy interpreted his whole literary career as an attempt to exorcise the ghost of a brutal father. Many literary biographies interpret writers as neurotics who, were it not for their writing, would have been helpless and unable to function (Blackmur, Hemingway, Kafka). Certainly most writers do not choose to write, but are driven and compelled to do it, need it desperately, find it indispensable. Ralph Ellison, in my one conversation with him, simply assumed this to be true: concerning the novelist we were discussing, he said, "I wonder what hurt him into writing." Similarly, John Gross speaks of "the artist's power of transforming private neurosis into meaningful public myth." And Auden in his "Letter to Lord Byron" wrote, "For no one thinks unless a complex makes him, / Or till financial ruin overtakes him."[8]

On the other hand, writing involves very serious psychological dangers: the lurking hope, conscious or unconscious, of fame, fortune, and love of women is impossible to eradicate, but fatal to over-indulge. Other mostly unconscious motives are: justification, exculpation: you

8. *Letters from Iceland* (New York: Random House, 1937), 234. (Auden dropped this section from later versions.)

try to justify yourself, show that it wasn't your fault, so you won't feel so rotten about yourself. Complicity: you try to make the reader share your guilt, give you permission. You try through reinterpretation and substitution to give your life meaning.

Perhaps the greatest psychological danger is that of developing a kind of divided consciousness, so that you assume a "spectator" stance, feel that nothing is real until written down and written about, that literature is more real than life, that the self is always and merely an onlooker. In this condition, you realize that you can't both live and write at the same time; you feel, in the classic philosophic dilemma, that you can't have enough time and energy for both, that you must choose between action and contemplation.

To put it in other terms, the problem is that you can't be a spectator and an actor at the same time. Shakespeare may be cited as having done it, since he was certainly a professional actor, at least in a small way; but the Sonnets and *The Tempest* are sufficient evidence that he agonized over the dilemma. As Adrienne Rich said, you have to decide whether you want to be the poet or the girl in the poem (unless, I should add, you are Elizabeth Barrett Browning). And this dilemma can't be resolved by vague talk about how quantum theory shows that observer and observed are not completely separate.

The artist, then, is not the ideal or normal man, but is in some ways closer to the madman or criminal (or con man, as in Thomas Mann's *Confessions of Felix Krull, Confidence Man*), or obsessive-compulsive at least, than to the well-rounded "wholesome" normal person. Notoriously, Plato excluded poets from his ideal republic, on the ground that they are liars, irresponsible and over-emotional, tending to be anarchic, stirrers up of strife. Aristotle answered, indirectly, that poets reveal universal and more important truths than historians, and that they produce a catharsis of the emotions they stir up, leaving the audience more stable. But in spite of Aristotle's persuasiveness, the Platonic suspicion that poets are not likely to be ideal citizens has never been put to rest entirely. As in Auden's "Unknown Citizen," the sociologist's or bureaucrat's ideal is not the same as the poet's. (In Auden's poem about Swarthmore people, "A Healthy Spot," beginning "They're nice . . . ," he contrasts the limitations of niceness with the demands of existential choice in the religious sense.) The artist—"that queer monster," as Henry James called him—is not the ideal, model, or paradigm for schoolchildren; he often is emphatically *not* nice.

Most of the fuss about making schoolchildren "creative" by letting them fingerpaint, play with clay, and write "poetry" is nonsense. It is just possible that it may give some a sense of the arts, may help produce an occasional artist, and so may not be always *wholly* nonsense. But it is certainly misleading to suggest that poets are no different from us, we all are poets, or should be; poetry is no big deal, but just another game; being creative is *such* fun. Compare Heine: "Aus meinen grossen Schmerzen / Mach ich die kleinen Lieder"; or Housman: "'Tis true, the stuff I bring for sale / Is not so brisk a brew as ale: / Out of a stem that scored the hand / I wrung it in a weary land." William Butler Yeats thinks of the artist as one who "has awakened from the common dream" and comments: "The rhetorician would deceive his neighbours, / The sentimentalist himself; while art / Is but a vision of reality."[9] In "Meru" Yeats further generalizes this contrast: civilization is "hooped together," given the "semblance of peace / By manifold illusion"; but man cannot cease from thought, "Ravening, raging, and uprooting that he may come / Into the desolation of reality" (287). Civilization is based upon illusion, and the artist sees through it.

Of course poets are not wholly different from us, the readers, or we could not read the poetry and see ourselves in it. But "confessional" poets and the revival of literary biography (and pathology) have made everyone aware of just how far from "normal" many writers have been: for example, among recent ones, Lowell, Plath, Sexton, Cheever, Faulkner, Berryman—some insane from time to time, alcoholic, homosexual, suicidal, others severely neurotic, variously crippled, needing their art to keep going. This is not to say the artist is always a cripple or a freak (though some certainly are), but that nothing is without its cost, least of all the gift of artistic talent.

The double nature of creative talent, both blessing and curse, gift and infection, as in the myths of Hephaestus or Philoctetes (interpreted

9. *Collected Poems* (New York: Macmillan, 1953), 159 ("Ego Dominus Tuus").

most fully in Edmund Wilson's *The Wound and the Bow*[10]), is, of course, one of the most ancient and heartfelt themes in poetry. Perhaps the best-known rendering is Milton's: if the poet can be cut off in his youth like Lycidas, then "Alas! what boots it with uncessant care / To tend the homely slighted shepherd's trade, / And strictly meditate the thankless Muse?" In lines that must strike a responsive chord in every writer's breast, he asks, "Were it not better done as others use, / To sport with Amaryllis in the shade, / Or with the tangles of Neaera's hair?" His answer, not terribly convincing to most of us nowadays, is ultimately religious: "Fame is the spur," but what matters is fame in heaven, not on earth; and the only satisfactory critic and audience ("perfect witness of all-judging Jove") is God. Nor would most writers be very happy with Lycidas's earthly reward of appointment as the genius of the shore. Writers less reclusive than Milton lament perennially with Pope: "Why did I write? What sin to me unknown / Dipt me in ink? My parents', or my own?" Would-be writers ("All Bedlam, or Parnassus") "Apply to me, to keep them mad or vain." Goldsmith sees Poetry fly the deserted village, "Dear charming Nymph, neglected and decried, / My shame in crowds, my solitary pride; / Thou source of all my bliss, and all my woe, / That found'st me poor at first, and keep'st me so." "Should Beauty blunt on fops her fatal dart / Nor claim the triumph of a lettered heart," even so, says Johnson, the poet comes to no good end. And thus many a poet, shivering in his garret, complains to his Muse even while he rejoices in her favor, suspecting that the gift for writing is really a curse, disease *(cacoethes scribendi),* compulsion, vice, obsession.

As Auden, Eliot, Tate, and many other moderns of anti-Romantic disposition have observed, the writer's vocation is no substitute for philosophy or religion: it cannot give meaning to life, or justify or redeem it. Though every aspiring writer naturally wants to be certified, baptized, anointed, told he is indeed a writer and does have talent, it is a mistake to think of the question in terms of either/or; there are many degrees and kinds of talent, manifested at different ages and stages; and there is no known litmus test. There is no Olympus for writers, where

10. *The Wound and the Bow: Seven Studies in Literature* (New York: Oxford University Press, 1947).

the godlike happy few look down on the struggling masses; no sharp division. Every good reader is a potential writer, as we have said. But the desire to be a writer doesn't make you one, and to think of yourself as a writer is often damaging psychologically: it may make you feel that nothing is real until it is written down, and this may produce a sense of unreality in daily life that is distorting and even dangerous.

Choosing writing as a vocation makes sense only if you can't help it, and if your motive is finally that you enjoy (in some sense, in spite of the pain of composition, of the whole process of writing) doing it for its own sake, or with the hope of living more fully, with heightened awareness and perceptiveness. Seen in this context, art for art's sake is thus a sensible doctrine. As Gross points out, there is a direct line from Arnold and Pater to Wilde and the aestheticism of the '90s, and "by appearing to surround the idea of culture with a devotional hush, Arnold helped to give it a bad name"; but Arnold's culture always embodied social concerns and Christian conceptions of charity and loving kindness; his conviction was that "no individual life can be truly prosperous, passed in the midst of men who suffer."

The writer is seen in Joyce's *Portrait of the Artist as a Young Man* as "a priest of eternal imagination, transmuting the daily bread of experience into the radiant body of everliving life." Stephen will "go to encounter for the millionth time the reality of experience and to forge in the smithy of my soul the uncreated conscience of my race." But Stephen sees himself as Icarus, sure to fall: "Old father, old artificer, stand me now and ever in good stead"; so there is in him a touch of the sacrificial victim, the poète maudit. Art, he knows, cannot be satisfactory as a substitute for religion; for the writer, his gift is curse more often than blessing.

Freud's view (or one of his views) is simplistic: it is not the whole or central truth that the writer wants what everyone wants—wealth, honor and fame, the love of women—and gets them by appearing to give them up to pursue his art. Writers' wants are more varied and elusive—for example, revenge against time, to preserve and record memory and personal experience, to recover the lost world of childhood (as in Jarrell, Wordsworth, Alain-Fournier in *Le Grand Meaulnes*), to be known and remembered as an individual.

Is every man (and woman and child) really a potential writer? The Romantic view (Rousseau, Blake, Wordsworth) was that every child is creative, and the artist is the ideal man, is what we would all become if we were not deformed, stunted, and frustrated by society and its institutions. In spite of the obvious absurdities it leads to, this view contains a germ of truth: every *good* reader does contain a potential writer, and it is through this potentiality, this kind of imagination, that he responds to literature. Of course, these readers could actually become writers only if they were willing to invest the time and effort required to learn the craft and art. Because of this potential in the reader, however, reader and writer share a kind of intimacy, a bond deeper than those of ordinary life. "Reader, I married him," confides Charlotte Brontë's Jane Eyre; the gentle reader can be counted on to understand and sympathize. Furthermore, as Proust says, "In reality every reader is, while he is reading, the reader of his own self. The writer's work is merely a kind of optical instrument which he offers to the reader to enable him to discern what, without this book, he would perhaps never have perceived in himself. And the recognition by the reader in his own self of what the book says is the proof of its veracity."[11]

Every good reader is indeed a latent or potential writer; only through this interest does he respond to literature; so reader and writer make common cause, share a common longing to communicate experience to others, tell how it is and how it was, express thoughts and feelings, and make something that will last, will preserve the identity and personality of the unique self. The difference between writer and would-be writer is one of degree, not kind: no art is ever completely successful or perfect, no writer ever entirely sure, when he finishes a work, that he will ever write again. The writer is "being a writer" only when actually writing, if then. But the common ground is that every reader, when he reads well, is a collaborator, exercising functions similar and analogous to those of the writer.

Almost everyone feels that his unique personality is precious and his thoughts and feelings are worth preserving. This nearly universal

11. Marcel Proust, *Remembrance of Things Past* (New York: Random House, 1981), 3:949.

yearning to express and preserve one's identity and personality is understandable; and to share experience with others, to make something lasting, is a noble ambition, basic to humanity. But it is hard to reconcile with the curious fact that nowadays far more people want to write poetry than want to read it; more people will submit manuscripts to every poetry contest than will read the winning poem. In the United States, at any rate, many of those who want to be writers have little interest in reading; and this mostly recent development is very disturbing.

Creative writing students need to read widely and deeply, not to read only each other. And reading from the writer's point of view is stimulating and liberating for the historical-critical student. Segregation of creative writing from the critical-historical study of literature makes academic study dull and trivial, and the creative writer self-absorbed, self-indulgent, and ignorant. It is always a mistake to separate the critic-reader-teacher-scholar-student too sharply from the writer. Much of the power of the New Criticism came from the fact that most of the critics were also poets, and they did not hesitate to interpret literature from the writer's point of view. In teaching, one can always feel a quickening of interest when students are asked to consider the problems facing the writer, to imagine themselves as writers. This is what "literature as literature" really means in practice. This kind of teaching makes students better readers, brings literature alive for them; and certainly writing courses should do this for them, whether or not they improve their writing.

This is a sharp contrast to the older view of the literature teacher as a kind of minor historian or genial appreciator, dealing in general knowledge and moral exhortation. It is unfortunate if English departments either withdraw into theory and history from the approach of writers or turn over teaching entirely to them. Obviously, writers can't teach entirely from the pragmatic or pseudo-professional point of view; they must also teach literature, including history and philosophy, so they need academics as much as academics need them. Ideal marriage is possible, though never easy. But we must aim at integration, not segregation. Separate but equal is not enough, though we must also remember that writers as people may have somewhat different needs and problems from academics.

To sum up, I have been concerned with serious writing, with aims beyond money or transient celebrity. Perhaps unnecessarily, I have warned against excessive expectations and reminded of inevitable costs. As businessmen say with such satisfaction, and I find myself repeating with embarrassment, there's no such thing as a free lunch. Nothing is without its costs, least of all writing; and (to repeat one of Auden's favorite apothegms) nothing in life is a substitute for anything else. On the other hand, I would leave you with the encouraging thought that, quite apart from any publication, the act of writing can be an aid to contemplation, can enhance perceptiveness and free the imagination, can increase awareness; and through all this enable the writer to be more alive. It can be, not a substitute for life, but a means to live more fully.

Auden once suggested that modern life, especially in the United States, made people feel anonymous and regimented, whereas the writer is an individual, free to express his identity and individuality, his "I" against the faceless mob. Hence people fearing the loss of their selves, their freedom and individuality, wish to be writers. Auden sympathized with this yearning, but was strongly opposed to the Romantic concept of the artist, of which this is probably a dim echo. The poet, Auden said, is a poet only while writing a poem, and he cannot know whether or not he will ever write another; at any other time he is a man like any other. This view, though refreshing in its deflation of the Romantic one, seems impossibly extreme; art requires a kind of *askesis,* a way of perceiving and thinking, as well as of working in a medium. Henry James advised, "Try to be one of the people upon whom nothing is lost," and spoke of "the very obvious truth that the deepest quality of a work of art will always be the quality of the mind of the producer. In proportion as that intelligence is fine will the novel, the picture, the statue partake of the substance of beauty and truth. . . . No good novel will ever proceed from a superficial mind."[12]

When Robert Giroux asked T. S. Eliot if he agreed that most editors are failed writers, Eliot replied, "Perhaps, but so are most writers."[13]

12. Leon Edel, ed., *The Future of the Novel* (New York: Vintage Books, 1956), 26.
13. Allen Tate, ed., *T. S. Eliot: The Man and His Work* (New York: Delacorte Press, 1966), 339.

Similarly, Ph.D.s and creative writers are both often writers manqué, but then so are most "successful" writers. The point is that it is a mistake to separate successful or talented writers from would-be writers too sharply and definitely. It is better to stress the common ground; no writer is always or wholly a successful writer. Auden liked to quote Valéry: "A poem is never finished, only abandoned."

Certainly the widespread desire to be a writer is often based on the expectation, conscious or unconscious, that being a writer will somehow give meaning to the writer's life, will justify his failings and defects; that his art will redeem his life. Proust is, of course, the grand archetype here, redeeming his life through translating it into art, triumphantly finding the lost time and recapturing the past in a great novel. Joyce's Stephen Dedalus rejects the Jesuit priesthood to become a priest of art, transubstantiating the bread of daily life into the supernatural richness and strangeness of art. But for most aspirant writers, there is no such definitive epiphany: if they succeed in writing a successful poem or novel or play, they proceed immediately to anxiety about what they should write next. The world seems remarkably unchanged by their accomplishment; fame, fortune, and happiness still elude them.

This belief, which sometimes appears to lurk at the bottom of almost everyone's heart, that to become a successful writer would justify all his failings and solve all his problems, is both absurd and pathetic. Nobody has more problems than writers: trying to write adds constantly to their anxiety about meeting their own expectations or those of others. So many never succeed in equaling again their first successful novel or play or volume of poems, and they struggle grimly against their feelings of frustration and embarrassment. Even more never succeed in writing anything at all that is recognized as successful, and they feel they have dedicated their lives to writing in vain.

As Flaubert observed, the writer sometimes feels that ordinary people are right after all ("Ils sont dans le vrai"), that what they have and he has given up for the solitary labors his art requires is finally most important. To repeat once more what Auden said, nothing in life is a substitute for anything else; there is no law of compensation. What is lost remains lost, what is sacrificed remains sacrificed. Even if his art should bring him fame and wealth, these are no substitute for a family and friends, the pleasures of ordinary life. An occasional writer appears to be so well rounded and well balanced and happy as hardly to leave room for the obsessive drive that major literary achievement seems to require. They are like the lawyer in Boswell who had tried to be a philosopher, "but, I don't know how, cheerfulness was always breaking in."[14] To reconcile the two aims requires a delicate balance indeed.

Almost everyone hopes and wants to believe that children and ordinary people whose taste is uncorrupted will naturally love good art, and that the opposition between popular and good art is artificial and false; but they remain aware also that much art is in fact essentially elitist, so difficult as fully to be understood by only a small minority. Yeats, in "What Is Popular Poetry?" argued that popular poetry—the oral art of the illiterate—and the advanced poetry of the aesthetes, the cliques—were essentially the same; but this was never very plausible, even in Ireland, and is even less so now. On the other hand, it is unquestionably true that all good readers of imaginative literature are potentially writers, because reading uses exactly the same emotional and imaginative faculties as writing, only in a less developed and more passive form. Were this not true, the reader could not identify so strongly with the writer, could not escape from himself, so to speak (though it is through developing a part of himself), could not participate in this powerful bond and thus escape loneliness and isolation. As Proust said, "Through art alone are we able to emerge from ourselves, to know what another person sees of a universe which is not the same as our own and of which, without art, the landscapes would remain as unknown to us as those that may exist in the moon. Thanks to art, instead of seeing one world only, our own, we see that world multiply itself and we have at our disposal as many worlds as there are original artists."[15] Kafka said poignantly, "A book should be an ax with which to attack the frozen sea within"; "Works of art are of an infinite loneliness, and by nothing to be understood so little as by criticism."

Many aspirant writers will never succeed in publishing—though as soon as I say this, I think of wildly improbable exceptions, such as

14. James Boswell, *The Life of Samuel Johnson, LL.D.* (New York: Oxford University Press, 1933), 2:230.
15. Proust, *Remembrance,* 3:932.

the seventy-year-old lady who wrote a best-selling first novel (Helen Santmyer, *And Ladies of the Club*), or J. K. Toole, whose mother got his *Confederacy of Dunces* published after his suicide by insistently bringing the manuscript to Walker Percy's attention, or J. R. Waller, Professor of Management, pushing the right buttons to manage the reading public. But this is not the point. The desire to write, whether or not it results in publication, is not a foolish or contemptible ambition. The difference between reader and writer, and between successful and unsuccessful writers, is not absolute but a matter of degree. The great writer is not basically different from other writers or from the ordinary reader; we should never forget the bonds of common humanity shared by all three. What they produce may be very different; but the processes involved are essentially the same.

As to publication, it is never as important to anyone else as to the author, and fame is so capricious and utterly unpredictable that he should try not to dream of it. Perhaps the greatest benefit of trying to write, with or without any success, is that it certainly will make you a better reader. In no other way can you see why masterpieces are written the way they are; what alternatives were possible; what the problems were and how the author solved them; in short, see the whole matter as it presented itself to the author, and exactly why and how he did what he did. This kind of understanding will almost certainly improve the craft and scope of your own writing, and will certainly give you a kind of sympathetic comprehension of great art that cannot be gained otherwise.

When we ask how those who have practiced the art with some substantial success feel about their vocation, we almost always get the same answer. However frustrated with practical results—economic, social, or personal—they may be, and however dissatisfied with their own accomplishments, most writers pay tribute to their art as a way of knowing and perceiving, as a discipline of living, and as a source of pleasure and satisfaction beyond any other. They may be uneasy sometimes at the dangers of art becoming a substitute for life, of the impossible attempt to be both spectator and actor, of the Muse replacing real mistresses; but they write finally because they can't help doing it and they love it and they desperately need it.

∽

CHAPTER 2

Cosmology

and the

Writer

MY TITLE SOUNDS faintly absurd, as if to suggest that cosmology may be the central problem for the aspiring writer. It might be more useful to discuss ecology for the respiring writer, tautology for the perspiring writer, or even theology for the expiring writer. Yet I do seriously want to explore the possible relations of writers and cosmology.

For earlier modern writers, from Baudelaire and Flaubert on, science was simply the enemy. Yeats felt a "monkish hate" for it because Huxley and Tyndall deprived him of the religion of his childhood, and Allen Tate made the case against Positivism in an impassioned lifelong polemic. Few writers now would take so extreme a view; science and technology have become so central to our lives that they must be taken into account. Still, I suspect that most writers feel a lingering suspicion, hostility, or at best indifference, toward science. They feel, as writers have always felt, that, admirable as its practical results may be, science doesn't deal with what is really most important. In *Paradise Lost,* the Archangel Raphael tells Adam that instead of wondering about celestial motions, he would do better to be "lowly wise" and cultivate

Sewanee Writers' Conference lecture, July 1993; published in *The Hudson Review,* spring 1994.

his garden. In *Rasselas* Dr. Johnson portrays a learned astronomer who says, piously, "To man is permitted the observation of the skies, but the practice of virtue is commanded." However, it develops that after forty years of observing the skies the astronomer has come to believe that he is responsible for controlling the weather—a kind of madness oddly anticipating the great John von Neumann's conviction that computers would enable us to predict and control the weather. (This is the same von Neumann who thought reason required the United States to make a preemptive nuclear strike on Russia.) Blake's "The atoms of Democritus / And Newton's particles of light / Are sands upon the Red Sea shore / Where Israel's tents do shine so bright" is, I take it, another expression of relative importance: even if true, the scientific vision is not what matters most.

As everyone knows who has read Stephen Hawking's *A Brief History of Time*[1]—and almost everyone seems to have read or seen or heard that phenomenal best seller—exciting discoveries about the size, age, and beginning of the universe, as well as about the nature of matter and of mind, have been made within the past few decades. A very brief summary of the main points may be useful. The big bang, paradigm of modern cosmology, was first given this derisive title by its principal opponent, Fred Hoyle; but the undignified name has survived respectability. The paradigm was predicted by Einstein, but he inserted a cosmological constant to keep the universe static (and later said this was his biggest mistake). The Russian Alexander Friedmann did not make this mistake, and developed a theoretical model of the expanding universe; the American astronomer Edwin Hubble observed the red shift in distant stars and produced conclusive evidence in 1929 that the universe is expanding and that ours is only one of many galaxies. Further and final confirmation from a different kind of evidence was provided in 1965 by the discovery by Penzias and Wilson of uniform microwave background radiation and the identification of it as the residue of the original explosion. When the theory was thus doubly confirmed, scientists had to take the big bang seriously.

1. Stephen W. Hawking, *A Brief History of Time: From the Big Bang to Black Holes* (Toronto and New York: Bantam Books, 1988).

That the earth is not the center even of our solar system has not been news since Copernicus. The significant new point is that the universe is not static, but expanding; its age therefore is intertwined with its size (to put it in layman's language; both are now established at about 15 billion years or light-years). By reversing Hubble's expanding universe, we can go back to the initial space-time singularity of infinite density and temperature, some 15 billion years ago. Interpreting the big bang is a fascinating challenge to scientists because it requires bringing together the two extremes of the macroscopic or large-scale structure of the universe governed by relativity theory and the submicroscopic world of subatomic particles governed by quantum theory. Many scientists hope that research in these areas, with the aid of such devices as the Hubble space telescope and the supercolliders, will result in a final theory explaining the relations of the four fundamental forces and encompassing both the vast universe now dealt with by relativity theory and the unimaginably tiny realm of the quantum.

I am neither a scientist nor a science and technology groupie (one of those who believe that literature and the book culture are doomed and the future belongs to virtual reality, artificial intelligence, holograms, and multimedia), but an intermittent student of the history and philosophy of science. (I find it comforting, by the way, that the word "scientist" was coined as late as 1840, by analogy with the word "artist"; before that practitioners of science were called merely natural philosophers.) I am not concerned in this talk with the speculative analogies between "creativity" in art and in science. Nor am I concerned primarily with the use of science as subject-matter for poetry or fiction, though this is a fascinating and amusing topic, and I confess that since childhood I have been an occasional addict of science fiction. My interest is in what the serious novelist or poet or playwright might gain from greater awareness of the recent developments in cosmology already mentioned and in biology, specifically neuroscience, the study of the brain in its relation to the mind.

Carl Sagan says in his introduction to Hawking's *Brief History:* "This is also a book about God . . . or perhaps about the absence of God. . . . Hawking is attempting, as he explicitly states, to understand the mind of God" (x). Sagan is here referring to Hawking's final paragraph, which suggests that if and when this final theory is discovered, "it should in time be understandable in broad principle by everyone, not just a few scientists. Then we shall all, philosophers, scientists, and just ordinary people, be able to take part in the discussion of the question of why it is that we and the universe exist. If we find the answer to that, it would be the ultimate triumph of human reason—for then we would know the mind of God" (175).

In "A Brief History of *A Brief History*" (*Popular Science*, August 1989, 70–72), Hawking remarks that if he had deleted this last sentence, as he almost did, it would have cut the sales of the book in half. Sagan's seizing on this point in his introduction shows his instinct for what will attract the popular mind; but Hawking seems to sense that this is a kind of deception. The book is, of course, about God only insofar as God is identified with the physical universe, or as the clock-maker "to wind up the clockwork and choose how to start it off" (140). (Clock-maker, however, is the wrong metaphor; the big bang would restore to God the thunder, to say the least!) But Hawking's sentence does suggest somewhat meretriciously a reconciliation of science and religion designed to appeal to the widespread yearning and therefore the enormous market for such reconciliations.

Freeman Dyson is like Hawking in being originally English and a renowned theoretical physicist; but in temperament and outlook he is a polar opposite. As to religion, he says, "I speak for myself alone. Any statement which attempted to express a consensus of scientists about religious and philosophical questions would miss the main point. . . . The voice of science is a Babel of diverse languages and cultures. . . . Many first-rate scientists are Christians . . . many are militant atheists, many are like me, loosely attached to Christian beliefs by birth and habit but not committed to any particular dogma."[2] He is rather scornful of extremes on both sides: the arrogant and old-fashioned "scientific materialism" of some biologists, and the claims to infallibility of some fundamentalists and Catholics.

Specifically, Dyson believes "that we are here to some purpose, that the purpose has something to do with the future, and that it transcends altogether the limits of our present knowledge and understanding. . . .

2. Freeman Dyson, *Infinite in All Directions* (New York: Harper & Row, 1988), 5.

If you like, you can call this transcendent purpose God. If it is God, it is a Socinian God, inherent in the universe and growing in power and knowledge as the universe unfolds. Our minds are not only expressions of its purpose but also contributions to its growth" (294). This is much like John Wheeler's concept of a "participatory universe," in which the evolution of subsequent observers through the act of observing the universe creates a texture of meaning that becomes the universe.

The anthropic principle (which is respectfully rejected by Hawking and embraced as meta-science by Dyson) is fully considered in *The Anthropic Cosmological Principle*.[3] The Copernican principle that man does not occupy a privileged position in the Universe must be qualified: "Our location in the Universe is necessarily privileged to the extent of being compatible with our existence as observers" (1). It is not true that man is unimportant in view of the enormousness of space and time: "The Universe needs to be as big as it is in order to evolve just a single carbon-based life form" (3). The Weak Anthropic Principle shows that "the observed structure of the Universe is restricted by the fact that we are observing the structure" (4). Its size is not random but determined by the constants of nature. "The sizes of atoms, people, and planets are not accidental, nor are they the inevitable result of natural selection" (359). The Strong Anthropic Principle is that the "Universe must be such as to admit the creation of observers within it at some stage" (6; that is, it could not have been different).

According to Barrow and Tipler, most biologists believe that man is unique, intelligence "an incredibly improbable accident," not necessarily an advantage in natural selection (124); only astronomers and some physicists think there is intelligent life on other planets (566). It is "simply untrue that there is nothing special about the epoch in which we now live. . . . We have shown at length that the epoch in which we live is very special in permitting the evolution of carbon life" (601).

Modern cosmologists have no interest in the argument from design. In the first place, evolution is a sufficient explanation; in the second, the argument from design could prove at most only that God exists,

3. John D. Barrow and Frank J. Tipler, *The Anthropic Cosmological Principle* (Oxford and New York: Oxford University Press, 1988).

not that he has any relation to mankind. Einstein, in spite of his talk about the Old One and God not playing dice and being subtle but not malicious, was and remained a thoroughgoing atheist and determinist. ("I believe in Spinoza's God who reveals himself in the harmony of all that exists, but not in a God who concerns himself with the fate and actions of men.")[4] The big bang does suggest a God with thunder, but the fundamentalists who advocate teaching creation science are not happy with it, because nothing after the Bang fits the biblical account. Peter Caws says, "The so-called argument from design assumes intelligent planning, and a great many people attribute to the Creator the really superior, the practically infinite intelligence that would be needed to produce the marvels that we find on all sides in the natural world. But consider where we get the idea of intelligence: the only cases of it we know, in full-fledged form, occur among human beings with functioning brains, and there is plenty of evidence that the intelligence really is linked to the brain."[5] If intelligence depends on the existence of the brain, we can hardly say that the emergence of the brain depended on intelligence.

James Trefil, in a different way, demystifies the notion of "creation": "As seen by modern physicists, matter is just one more form of energy, a form which can be shifted around at will. Seen in this light, the creation of the universe is no more miraculous than the operation of an ordinary nuclear reactor. Both are just examples of the basic equivalence of matter and energy." At first, "the universe was a vacuum full of evanescent matter. Then, quite by accident, enough fluctuations occurred close enough together to trigger the process by which energy is drained from the gravitational field, and the process of runaway inflation started. . . . When the period of inflation was over, the Big Bang had begun and, as they say, the rest is history." He quotes another physicist as saying, "The universe is simply one of those things that happen from time to time."[6]

4. Nigel Calder, *Einstein's Universe* (New York: Viking Press, 1979), 138.

5. Peter Caws, *Yorick's World: Science and the Knowing Subject* (Berkeley: University of California Press, 1993), 78.

6. James Trefil, *Reading the Mind of God* (New York: Scribner's, 1989), 212.

What has cosmology meant to aspiring writers in the past? How important has it been to them? While a systematic survey would be tedious, it may be worthwhile to look at a few examples. The Presocratics remind us that it was once possible to be simultaneously scientists, philosophers, and poets: T. S. Eliot was inspired by them, especially by Heraclitus, in *Four Quartets,* in the themes of time and the transformation of the four elements, and Gerald Edelman takes his title from Empedocles for his latest book, *Bright Air, Brilliant Fire: On the Matter of the Mind* (1992).

Lucretius was, after the Presocratics, the first and greatest poet of cosmology. Though Lucretius was not much interested in science for its own sake, and expounded the doctrine of Epicurus, who was himself more philosopher than scientist, both used the atomic theory of Leucippus and Democritus as a scientific basis. Actually, Lucretius is not much concerned with the details of cosmology; his central points are that there is nothing out there but atoms and the void, and that eclipses are natural phenomena, not supernatural omens. While the gods do exist, they are not visible and have nothing to do with the heavenly bodies or with human beings. There must be, he thinks, many inhabited worlds; earth and man are not unique.

He is a great advocate of science because he believes with total conviction that his gospel of scientific materialism will banish "this terror then, this darkness of the mind": fear of death and what lies after it: eternal punishment, hell, ghosts, the unknown. So he proclaims with passion that all passion is bad and that religion is the chief source of man's unhappiness (the reverse, we note, of the modern notion of religion as consolation). He sets out to prove that there is absolutely nothing out there but atoms and the void: no ghosts or spirits or gods (or rather, the gods do exist, but are completely indifferent to man).

Dante's cosmos is Ptolemaic, but traditionally and theologically symbolic. From earth (with hell at the center) we rise through water, air, and fire to the three infrasolar spheres of the Moon, Mercury, and Venus, representing inconstancy, ambition, and love, imperfect versions of the theological virtues of faith, hope, and charity, imperfect because in the shadow of the earth. After the Sun we encounter Mars, Jupiter, and Saturn, representing the cardinal virtues of fortitude, justice, and temperance. Then come the fixed stars, representing the Church Triumphant; the Crystalline or Primum Mobile, representing the angelic orders; and the Empyrean, which contains the Trinity, the Virgin, angels, and saints, but is really beyond space and time, and is where all the spirits really are.

Milton's universe is similar, but looser and not static; it is not complete to begin with, but much of it is under construction during *Paradise Lost,* in response to events in the poem. Hell is prepared for the fallen angels as they fall; they build Pandaemonium for themselves. When Satan flies to the newly created World (Milton's term for the whole Ptolemaic cosmos), he sees it hanging by a golden chain from Heaven, which is in size like the moon compared to the smallest star. Satan travels through the traditional Ptolemaic spheres of the World to reach Earth at its center. Later, Adam inquiring of celestial motions is given a lecture by Raphael explaining why the Earth, though smallest and farthest from Heaven, may nevertheless be the most important of these bodies. The archangel then advises Adam to concern himself with more important things; it doesn't really matter, he says, whether the Sun or the Earth is center. (He does, however, remark that the Ptolemaic cycles and epicycles are needlessly complicated, and gives a broad hint that the Copernican theory may well be true: "What if the sun / Be center to the World, and other stars / By his attractive virtue and their own / Incited, dance about him various rounds?") After Adam and Eve sin, Sin and Death build a broad causeway from Hell through Chaos to the World.

The doctrine opposite to Lucretius's, that the design of the universe proves the existence of a Designer, is exemplified by Addison's ode "The spacious firmament on high," with its thesis that the heavenly bodies proclaim, "The hand that made us is divine." But even in Addison's day, the contemplation of the Newtonian cosmos often led—as in Pope's *Essay on Man*—to minimally consoling thoughts: yes, the design proves the existence of a designer, but not that the designer cares anything for man. The clock-maker god can't intervene in his clockwork. The worst error of human pride, Pope says, is to think the universe made for man, or his world the only one or the most important. Like many other theodicies, Pope's *Essay on Man* denounces anthropocentrism as the worst manifestation of human pride, an attempt to upset divine order by breaking the great chain of being.

The most effective poetic uses of cosmology in later poetry have been based on images derived from Dante or Milton. For example, George Meredith's great sonnet "Lucifer in Starlight," which revives Milton's Satan, restores him to his prelapsarian status as Lucifer, and launches him on a flight around the modern world:

> On a starred night Prince Lucifer uprose.
> Tired of his dark dominion swung the fiend
> Above the rolling ball in cloud part screened,
> Where sinners hugged their spectre of repose.

But he is defeated by the laws of modern science:

> He reached a middle height, and at the stars,
> Which are the brain of heaven, he looked, and sank.
> Around the ancient track marched, rank on rank,
> The army of unalterable law.

Similarly, William Empson (who took a Cambridge First in Mathematics as well as in English—surely the only poet who ever did so?) evokes the Dantean cosmos in "Legal Fiction," fusing it with modern real estate law:

> Law makes long spokes of the short stakes of men . . .
> Your rights extend under and above your claim
> Without bound; you own land in Heaven and Hell; . . .
> Your rights reach down where all owners meet, in Hell's
> Pointed exclusive conclave, at earth's centre
> And up, through galaxies, a growing sector.
> . . . the lighthouse beam you own
> Flashes, like Lucifer, through the firmament.
> Earth's axis varies, your dark central cone
> Wavers, a candle's shadow, at the end.

Empson's "To an Old Lady" may well be the only good poem based on astronomy (more or less modern in this case), and specifically on the possibility of space flight to another inhabited planet of the solar system (it would have to be specifically Mars). The old lady, who appears to be a relative of the poet, lives in another, older, world of time, customs and manners; it may be observed but not invaded:

> Ripeness is all; her in her cooling planet
> Revere; do not presume to think her wasted.
> Project her no projectile, plan nor man it. . . .
> Our earth alone given no name of god
> Gives, too, no hold for such a leap to aid her.
> . . . No, to your telescope; spy out the land;
> Watch while her ritual is still to see,
> . . . Stars how much further from me fill my night.
> Strange that she too should be inaccessible,
> Who shares my sun. He curtains her from sight,
> And but in darkness is she visible.

Empson's "The World's End" is one of the few successful poems about relativity, contrasting its cosmos with the Miltonic and with extravagant Romantic imagery:

> Fly with me then to all's and the world's end
> And plumb for safety down the gaps of stars
> . . . Alas, how hope for freedom, no bars bind;
> Space is like earth, rounded, a padded cell;
> Plumb the stars' depth, your lead bumps you behind;
> Blind Satan's voice rattled the whole of Hell.
> . . . Apple of knowledge and forgetful mere
> From Tantalus too differential bend.
> The shadow clings. The world's end is here.
> This place's curvature precludes its end.

Most other poems about Einsteinian space are essentially jokes, like Cummings'

> Space being (don't forget to remember) Curved
> (and that reminds me who said o yes Frost
> Something there is which isn't fond of walls)

. . . of Course life being just a Reflex you
know since Everything is Relative or

to sum it All Up god being Dead (not to

mention inTerred)
                            LONG LIVE that UPwardlooking
Serene Illustrious and Beatific
Lord of Creation, MAN: . . .

MacLeish's "The End of the World" is similarly a joke, if a grim one:
in the middle of the circus

Quite unexpectedly the top blew off:

And there, there overhead, there, there, hung over
Those thousands of white faces, those dazed eyes,
. . . There in the sudden blackness the black pall
Of nothing, nothing, nothing—nothing at all.

Yeats is the only poet whose use of astrology has been really effective;
this is so because he believed in it deeply, and his belief gives a magical
power to poems about time and myth, such as "Leda," "The Second
Coming," and many others. The astrological meanings are not explicit,
but submarine, just below the surface; the reader does not have to
be aware of them to get the effect of mingled fear and exultation: that
vast and mysterious significances are in question, events of tremendous
importance are happening.

Other visionary poets, like James Dickey in *The Zodiac*, affirm the
ultimate analogy, or identity, of the poetic imagination and the divine
power that created the stars; but for them, too, the astrological zodiac
offers much better imagery for the purpose than scientific cosmology.
Dickey also wrote a good poem on the Apollo moon landings, again
using mainly classical mythology.

Refusing to be intimidated by traditional sublimity, Auden could say
cheerfully, "Looking up at the stars, I know quite well / That for all they
care, I can go to hell," and Robert Penn Warren that the stars are "only

a backdrop for / The human condition" and the sky "has murder in the eye, and I / Have murder in the heart, for I / Am only human. We look at each other, the sky and I. / We understand each other."

Robert Pack in his poems based on the books of Heinz Pagels, *Before it Vanishes, A Packet for Professor Pagels* (1989), suggests an implicit comparison to Dante. Pack usually imagines Pagels as a kind of guide-companion, like Virgil to Dante, or as a friend (like Lucretius's Memmius) whom he is addressing; but the tone is mostly comic. Pack's book prefaces each poem by a quotation from Pagels: the poem then tells a story or presents a scene that parallels or contrasts to the passage from Pagels. The plan is brilliant, but, except for the dramatic ending when Pack bids farewell to Pagels, who has fulfilled his own premonition of falling to his death while mountain climbing, the poems tend to be no more than pleasant or mildly amusing.

So what use can modern cosmology be to poets? Most poems inspired by it, aside from some of those mentioned, tend to be essentially jokes or light verse at best. The big bang is unimaginable, as is quantum reality; they can be represented only in numbers and mathematical structures. Astronomical distances—light years, parsecs, astronomical units—are beyond the human scale; we cannot really imagine them. The only cosmologies that work for the human imagination are symbolic, and the greatest are those of Dante and Milton; later poets have been most effective when they have alluded to or played off these in some manner.

What, then, have the new discoveries in cosmology to offer the aspiring fiction writer? Not much more than they offer the poet, I fear. No one, to my knowledge, has written well about the big bang, black holes (though the concept of total negation swallowing even light would seem to have interesting metaphorical possibilities), cold dark matter, the inflationary universe; nor, on the other hand, about the submicroscopic world of quantum reality. It is hard to see how anyone could. Both these extremes are beyond the human imagination; it is probably a mistake even to try to imagine them. As Peter Caws puts it,

> Everything we have learned about science suggests that away from the normal macroscopic center of things we can't form a perceptual model of it at all. We have grown up in what I call the "flat region"—a metaphor I

take from the fact that the earth seems flat where we live and we need to go off into space, or make geographical inferences of one sort or another, to conclude that it is round. So in the direction of the very large, the very fast, the very distant, the very small, we can only have mathematical models of how it really is.[7]

Certain other areas of science, such as biology and physiology, have much more promise: they can be used in what is perhaps the basic enterprise of most serious science fiction: defining the human. The assumption of many advocates of artificial intelligence that the mind is nothing more than a computer, and hence that computers can eventually become intelligent and conscious in the same sense as human beings, has been the basis of much entertaining science fiction. But recent studies of the brain such as those of Gerald Edelman and narrative case histories like those of Oliver Sacks have shown just how different the human brain is from a computer. At the same time that they eliminate scores of robots, androids, and superhuman computers from the possibilities of fiction, these books should be stimulating to good writers. They make clear how individual and far from mechanical human memory and perception are; as natural products of evolution, the brain and mind belong to biology rather than to physics.

The older naturalism that was the most obvious effect of a "scientific" viewpoint and dominated such novelists as Hardy, Zola, and Dreiser tended to produce a picture of human life that might be drab and depressing, but was at least solid and realistic. The alarming trend now is the opposite: in pop culture unrestricted fantasy seems all the rage, as in Broadway musicals, TV shows like *Quantum Leap,* and innumerable movies about minds transposed between children and adults or men and women. Apparently pop-psych books encouraging sexual fantasy as a good thing, South American magic realism, comic books and animated cartoons, and the ever-expanding technical possibilities of movies and TV have contributed to this phenomenon; but the basic source seems to be a vague notion in the popular mind that relativity and quantum theory, together with the uncertainty principle and

7. Caws, *Yorick's World,* 346.

speculation about alternative universes and time travel, have made it impossible to tell what is real. Tributaries like New Age thought, the mysterious East, and UFOs all flow into this river, where the Dancing Wu Li Masters practice the Tao of Physics and quantum healing takes care of health. All this might seem to be harmless liberation of the child within us, but what it tends to produce, both in visual media and in fiction, is an increasing reliance on spectacular special effects to get and retain the audience's attention.

The fact is what it has always been: that nothing in a story is interesting for more than a casual moment unless the audience believes it, unless the characters are recognizably like us in essential ways and their predicaments, desires, loves, and hates can be related to our own. Fantasy must be limited: if there are no limits to the strange powers of Superman or telepaths or omnipotent aliens, there are no rules to the game and therefore no interest (at least to those beyond the age of six). A sense of reality, a suspension of disbelief, is as necessary as ever to producing a successful narrative: not gritty realism or depressing naturalism, necessarily, but a sense that the characters are people like us in situations we might conceivably be in. Otherwise, the reader cannot identify with the characters.

Science, then, might help the fiction writer define the limits of imaginable reality and of the human as opposed to imaginable other forms of life. It may be immensely stimulating to the imagination. It might also improve his sense of fact, though the example of Thomas Pynchon makes this somewhat dubious: Pynchon's considerable knowledge of science does not prevent him from constantly blurring the line between fictional reality and fantasy, a blurring that reaches an extreme in his latest novel, *Vineland* (1990). In *Gravity's Rainbow* (1973), Pynchon made the most impressive use of science and technology that any recent novelist has achieved—not primarily cosmology, perhaps, but involving concepts like entropy and relativity, as the title suggests. As with such other novelists as Don DeLillo, however, Pynchon's obsession with paranoiac conspiracies prevents any sharp definition of reality.

But science is fictionally workable in such novels as Michael Crichton's *Jurassic Park,* where genetics, biology, and paleontology provide a means that is just barely possible in theory (cloning from DNA found in the blood of fossilized mosquitoes preserved in amber to resurrect dinosaurs and other creatures of the Jurassic era) to make an interesting novel of suspense and contemporary social satire (wicked scientists, unscrupulous entrepreneurs who wish to profit from the greatest of all theme parks). Alan Lightman's *Einstein's Dreams* has, somewhat surprisingly, become a best-seller; it is a well-informed fantasy based on Einstein's biography, imagining dreams Einstein might have had based on his theories of time and conversations he might have had with his friend Besso. But it isn't really a novel at all.

Perhaps the best science fiction novel yet written is Ursula Le Guin's *The Dispossessed* (1974), which involves cosmology only insofar as it is set on an earthlike planet with an inhabited moon—inhabited by all the idealistic radicals who have been exiled there. It is a fine novel, but the science is primarily anthropology, sociology, and politics. Carl Sagan's recent novel, *Contact* (1985), is about contact with extraterrestrials through wormholes (in theory barely conceivable), and Richard Powers's *The Gold Bug Variations* (1991) is a brilliant novel about a scientist and more centrally about science itself. It deals mainly with the discovery of the genetic code; its characters are a female reference librarian, a male molecular biologist who did early research on DNA, his female lover, and a dilatory young male art historian. The real subject, however, is the four-part structure of everything from the intertwining two couples to Bach fugues to the double helix of DNA and the four-part harmony of the universe.

Stephen Weinberg's notion of a final theory, justifying the need for a superconducting supercollider, is almost as arrogant as Hawking's assertion that final theory would reveal the Mind of God. Weinberg, in an editorial in the *New York Times,* professes exactly the same aim as Lucretius: final theory would banish such superstitions as astrology and creationism. But Weinberg also makes the sweeping statement that science provides the only truth man can attain, so should be sought for its own sake. No one nowadays would deny the immense importance of science and technology in our daily lives nor the impossibility of understanding the modern world without understanding them; but the claim of exclusive validity for scientific truth is fortunately now rather unusual.

The greatest physicists have had no delusions of omniscience. Newton described himself as "like a boy playing on the sea shore, and diverting myself in now and then finding a smoother pebble or a prettier shell than ordinary, while the great ocean of truth lay all undiscovered before me."[8] Einstein freed himself "from the chains of the 'merely personal,' dominated by wishes, hopes, and primitive feelings," through the study of science: "Out yonder there was this huge world, which exists independently of us human beings and which stands before us like a great, eternal riddle, at least partially accessible to our inspection and thinking. The contemplation of this world beckoned like a liberation."[9] As Peter Caws says,

> It is not so much that a Newtonian paradigm has been displaced by an Einsteinian one . . . —indeed, Newton *hasn't* been displaced, except at the remote fringes of conceptual possibility—it's rather that Newton never covered even his own domain in the way Laplace thought. Newton could give a complete account of how two massive bodies would interact in an otherwise empty universe, and the whole success of Newtonian science has consisted in pretending that real events can be represented as aggregates of independent pairwise interactions. . . . But Newton couldn't, and science still can't, give a complete account of how *three* massive bodies would interact, even in an otherwise empty universe.
>
> If science can't even solve the three-body problem in mechanics, its most elementary branch, how can anyone ever have thought that it could mirror the whole of nature? . . . The assumption that total discursive adequacy was what science claimed (rather than being what some immoderate scientists and their admirers claimed) has obscured the genuine lesson that science has to teach.[10]

It is worth noting that, though the assertion has been made often and confidently for more than three centuries that there are many planets orbiting other suns, no planet outside our solar system has yet been

8. Charles Singer, *A Short History of Scientific Ideas to 1900* (Oxford: Oxford University Press, 1959), 288.

9. Heinz R. Pagels, *The Cosmic Code* (New York: Bantam Books, 1983), 22.

10. Caws, *Yorick's World,* 360.

detected. (The perturbations in the image of Barnard's Star, the nearest to us, seem to have been caused not by an unseen companion but by defects in the telescope.) The appropriately named Hubble space telescope that is now in orbit will, it is hoped, eventually settle the question. But the first year of observations from the Hubble orbiting telescope (once it was properly corrected) has answered few, if any, questions; instead, it has raised new ones. It has provided further evidence that about 90 percent of the mass of the universe cannot be accounted for by present methods: perhaps it consists of invisible cold dark matter or some unknown form of matter (large soft atoms?) or enormous black holes; or perhaps our methods of computation are wrong. The latest data suggest that the universe may be only six billion years old, but equally valid data place some individual stars at sixteen billion—an intolerable contradiction. And no other solar system has yet been found, though there are various indications of similar phenomena in the process of birth or death. It is also worth noting that, though QED (quantum electrodynamics) is the most successful branch of modern physics in that it works beautifully, allowing accurate prediction and operation—it is the basis of the whole electronics industry, among many other things—the great physicist Richard Feynman, who pioneered in discovering and explaining its operation and uses, was fond of saying that nobody really understands it.

For me, at least, science fiction has lost most of its attraction as its favorite themes have been ruled out as contrary to fact: it is now definite that no intelligent life exists in our solar system, and no planet, much less a habitable one, has been discovered yet anywhere else. If any are discovered they will certainly be too distant for any communication other than radio. UFOs unfortunately do not exist. The strong probability, like it or not, is that man is unique in the universe. So the central theme of much science fiction—encounter with alien life-forms—is no longer plausible. In their fascinating debate, *Are We Alone?* Trefil and Rood say,

> Since the Copernican revolution the main thrust of science has been to make the assumption of mediocrity seem more and more reasonable. The earth is not at the center of the universe, but revolves around the sun.

The sun is a single star in a galaxy of 10 billion stars, and the galaxy itself is only one of millions in the universe. Darwin showed us that humanity has been created in the same way as other animals, and Freud showed us that there is more of the primitive in our nature than we might have thought. It seemed that the more we learned about ourselves, the less special we became.

Now, for the first time in five hundred years, things seem to be going the other way. During the past two decades, the more we have learned, the more we can see the earth as something special.[11]

The earth is a planet in the system of a single G star; is in the narrow band about that single G star where water will neither boil nor freeze for the billions of years necessary to produce life; has a large moon, which means there are large and variable tides, leading to numerous tidal pools; and the tilt of the earth's axis is just enough so that, in conjunction with the influence of the other planets, periodic changes in the climate occur. "Although the probability of any one of these features being present on a planet may not be impossibly small, the probability that all four will be present at the same time is. So maybe the earth *is* special, after all," Trefil says (125). On this particular bit of rock, circling this particular sun,

all of the millions of factors happened to work themselves out so that the first fragile molecules had enough time to form complicated chains, and these chains were given just the right amount of protection to form simple living systems, and these living systems changed their environment in just the right way so as to narrowly escape twin catastrophes and put oxygen into the atmosphere. This in turn allowed life to emerge onto land, and since the planet's orbit was just right, the weather changed, forcing the apelike creatures on the African savannah to build tools, fashion shelters, and start to think about the world around them.

If I were a religious man, I would say that everything we have learned about life in the past twenty years shows that we are unique, and therefore special in God's sight. Instead I shall say that what we have learned shows that it matters a great deal what happens to us. We are

11. Robert T. Rood and James S. Trefil, *Are We Alone? The Possibility of Extraterrestrial Civilizations* (New York: Scribner's, 1981), 124–25.

not the snail darters of the galaxy—one more life form whose ultimate fate is of little moment in the grand scheme of things. If we succeed in destroying ourselves, it will be a tragedy not only for the human race but for the entire galaxy, which will have lost the fruit of a 15-billion-year experiment in the formation of sentient life (252).

Writers can learn more about human nature from such humane scientists as these, and perhaps have their consciousnesses expanded by awareness of the new cosmology. But if what finally emerges is that man and his earth are unique in the universe, this is no surprise. Writers have always known that man (and woman) are unique on this earth. We share much, but not everything, with the animals; what writers have always explored with most fascination is what is not shared.

Auden mythologized the human realm as that of Clio, Muse of History, overlapping with but distinct from the realm of Dame Kind, or Mother Nature. In the light of this distinction, Hawking's title—*A Brief History of Time*—is a misnomer: time, in the cosmological sense, has no history; history pertains only to what has human significance. The big bang is noise, part of nature; what is peculiarly human is language or silence. Awareness of recent cosmology, then, may be of some help to the aspiring writer in his central enterprise of exploring what it is to be human and defining the boundaries of his unique domain.

CHAPTER 3

~

Sewanee

and Its

Writers

IT IS NOT UNUSUAL for a university to seem at odds with its surroundings: consider, for example, Princeton in the industrialized marshlands of New Jersey, the University of Chicago in its urban slums, Oxford among its factories. But the University of the South, isolated on a mountain in the Tennessee backwoods, seems even more incongruous with its location than these other monuments of collegiate Gothic. There has been, from the beginning, a stronger element of fantasy in its conception and history, giving it a peculiar ontological status, or—to put it more plainly—making it often seem not quite real. Hence it has suggested even more readily than these other universities the dimension and realm of myth. Let us glance briefly at its history, which explains why its dreaming spires were quite literally the home of forsaken beliefs, impossible loyalties, and lost causes.

Chartered in 1858, with grandiose but, at the time, entirely feasible plans to establish a "Southern Oxford" to rival the best of the world's universities, the University of the South acquired, to start with, the largest campus in America (ten thousand acres). (It was and is not, however, merely a campus but a domain wholly owned by the Southern

Based on a lecture given at the Sewanee Writers' Conference in July 1991.

dioceses of the Episcopal Church and ruled by a vice-chancellor with feudal powers.) When its six-ton marble cornerstone was laid in 1860, nine bishops, fifty other clergymen, and an audience of five thousand assembled in the wilderness to celebrate the occasion. But when it opened its doors in 1868, the contrast of actual fact with the original plans seemed melodramatic. The endowment of a half-million dollars had been lost in Confederate investments. Instead of a faculty of international distinction there were four amateur professors and nine grammar-school students; instead of splendid and elegant buildings there were a few ramshackle frame shanties. This contrast seems to us tragic and ironic. The irony, however, was not appreciated at the time, for the grinding, hardscrabble poverty was all too real. Sewanee, like the whole South, lived for many years thereafter in the shadow of the war; few literary seeds sprouted in this barren ground. As the South Carolina newspaper bard J. Gordon Coogler lamented, "Poor South! Her books get fewer and fewer; / She was never much given to literature."

A happy exception to Coogler's gloomy view was Sarah Barnwell Elliott, daughter of one of the founding bishops, who came to Sewanee to live in 1870, when she was twenty-two, and left for New York in 1895, having established a national reputation as novelist and writer of short stories, plays, biographies, and articles. She also established a reputation at Sewanee as the object of romantic adoration by generations of young men, though she never married.

Her writing was not the kind of sentimental and nostalgic local color stuff that was popular in the South, but was comparatively realistic and dealt often with such disturbing matters as racial and economic problems, lynching, dueling, politics, and the situation of women. Hence she was largely ignored in the South outside Sewanee; her reputation flourished mainly in New York and abroad. In the 1880s and 1890s her novels (*Jerry,* 1891, was the most popular) were published by the best New York publishers, and her stories and articles appeared in the leading national magazines.

Like her father, Miss Elliott was much concerned to improve the lot of blacks and of women, and she was an activist for women's rights: she led the suffrage movement in Tennessee, which was the only Southern state to ratify the Nineteenth Amendment. In her short stories these concerns are especially apparent; a selection of them, *Some Data and Other Stories of Southern Life,* was reprinted in 1981. Her letters and miscellaneous writings (preserved in the Sewanee archives) are sharply intelligent and very entertaining. For the 1900 student annual, she wrote about her recollections of Sewanee in the very early days:

> For a long time we were shut away here unheeded and unheeding. We liked ourselves, we enjoyed associating with ourselves; we were sorry for people who did not understand and appreciate Sewanee. . . . The next sign of progress did, however, cause a murmur; a little murmur, a friendly murmur, but still a murmur. It was when Dr. DuBose built Palmetto Hall. It was *so* large! And the plan for the University was that the students should be housed in small numbers, no one being allowed more than twelve. It is true that one lady had been allowed sixteen, and another had eighteen, but this hall was to have thirty! . . . We should be glad that our green, shady paths have broadened into roads, even though we do not admire the ruts and the red clay. The green paths were beautiful and romantic, but the roads mean traffic, and maybe some day these very roads will be leveled and graveled and be made as beautiful as roads can be. We miss the old simplicity, the dropping in informally for dinner or tea, or even breakfast. . . . We miss the walking parties, the ox-wagon picnics, the exploring expeditions down into the caves and valleys, the professors and students all walking and talking and laughing in company.[1]

However mythopoeic its topography may be, and however suggestive its early history, Sewanee would probably have had few writers but for one remarkable initiative, from which all her subsequent literary traditions and connections derive. This was the founding in 1892 of the *Sewanee Review.* Though the establishment of a press and a literary magazine had been part of the original grandiose plans for the university, it was an astonishing thing at this time for the faculty of a small, new, and still impoverished liberal arts college in the South to undertake and continue such an enterprise. As the masthead justly claims, the *Sewanee Review* is America's oldest literary quarterly continuously published under the same title.

1. Lily Baker et al., *Sewanee* (Sewanee, Tenn., 1932), 106–8.

Old Sewanee had obvious material and academic limitations, but this feat provides impressive evidence of its respect for intellectual and literary values. This may be partly explained by the university's relation to the Episcopal Church, which—because its services are (or were until very recently) based on the sixteenth-century Book of Common Prayer—has traditionally inculcated a feeling for the beauty of the English language, familiarity with the rhythms of poetry and prose, and respect for literature. The church connection has also protected the University of the South—in spite of its name—from too narrow a regionalism: some of the founding bishops were Northerners, most of the money was raised in England, and close connections with the church in England and in the North have always been maintained. In some respects, Sewanee has always been a kind of island or enclave in Tennessee.

The story of the *Review* begins with the arrival of William Peterfield Trent at Sewanee in 1888. Trent was a cocky, outspoken, and extremely independent young man of twenty-six. He was dyspeptic and, he said, "anti–ante-bellum"; many thought him arrogant and supercilious, though unquestionably very intelligent and energetic. He was notoriously an agnostic and opposed to the Old South myth: he denounced slavery, states' rights, and Southern chivalry. He did not much like England or the English. Later, he was outspokenly opposed to the Spanish-American War (though a lifelong friend of Theodore Roosevelt) and to World War I (in 1915 he wrote and published a poem praising German civilization).

Sewanee deserves much credit for hiring such a difficult and highly gifted young man in the first place, and then for continuing to support him in what must often have seemed subversive activities. Sewanee was then, in 1888, only twenty years old as a going institution; two former Confederate generals, Kirby-Smith and Shoup, were still teaching, and General Gorgas had only recently left Sewanee to become president of the University of Alabama.

In 1892, at the age of thirty, Trent published *William Gilmore Simms* in the American Men of Letters series, an important book still read and respected today. There was a great outcry over *Simms* from Charleston especially, but also from all over the South, because Trent was critical both of Simms and of the antebellum South. He dared to say that the Civil War was about slavery and slavery was wrong, also that Simms was rejected by Charleston society and that he, like other Southern writers, was greatly handicapped by the intellectual limitations of Southern culture. Trent called Charleston's leading class in Simms's time "a blind, exclusive, and thoughtless aristocracy"; and he extended this description to the entire antebellum South.[2] Life in the Southern states afforded "few opportunities to talents that did not lie in certain beaten grooves. It was a life gaining its intellectual nourishment, just as it did its material comforts, largely from abroad,—a life that choked all thought and investigation that did not tend to conserve existing institutions and opinions, a life that rendered originality scarcely possible except under the guise of eccentricity" (37). Of the antebellum Southern writer Trent says: "The models before him were those of statesmen and men of action. . . . Besides, he had no critics, no audience whose applause was worth having. His easy verses were received with a smile by his friends or with extravagant praise by an editor only too glad to fill his columns." He quoted Simms's final denunciation of Charleston, which "has never smiled on any of my labors, which has steadily ignored my claims, which has disparaged me to the last, has been the last place to give me its adhesion, to which I owe no favor, having never received an office, or a compliment, or a dollar at her hands" (148, 239). Of Simms Trent concluded, "Perhaps there has never been a man whose development was so sadly hampered by his environment."

Sewanee, where Trent had become the most popular teacher, supported him against the rising tide of criticism: later in 1892 he was made Professor of English and Acting Professor of History and Political Science, and Vice-Chancellor Gailor added a note of grateful appreciation of his work. Trent also, more significantly, found support and encouragement for his project of establishing a magazine. His most important friend and supporter was a remarkable young professor of Greek, Benjamin Wiggins, about Trent's own age, who took the main business responsibility for the magazine and who became

2. William Peterfield Trent, *William Gilmore Simms* (Boston and New York: Houghton, Mifflin, 1892), 20.

vice-chancellor in the following year. Wiggins, from South Carolina, had graduated from Sewanee in 1882 and later returned as professor of Greek. He studied at Hopkins (he was a pupil of the great Basil Gildersleeve and brought him to Sewanee to teach for three summers) and at Oxford. He became vice-chancellor in 1893. His sudden death at Commencement in 1909 marked the end of Sewanee's golden age, which began in the 1890s; the university soon thereafter closed its departments of medicine, law, nursing, engineering, and dentistry and had hard times financially for the next three decades. .

The idea of the *Sewanee Review* came from Trent's study of the periodicals with which William Gilmore Simms was connected. As Trent put it later,

> my work on the "Life of Simms" brought me in contact with the Southern Quarterly, and other old Southern Reviews, and the criticism my book received emphasized the fact that the South not only needed a literary organ but was less fortunate in that respect than it had been before the war. I also felt that current magazines throughout the whole country did little to supply the kind of literature that the English quarterlies gave England, and I saw no reason why the economic and political quarterlies then being published by our universities could not be paralleled in the field of literature. Besides, and this is quite important, The University of the South Magazine a year or two before had been quite successful in a literary way, but hardly as a students' organ. . . . This last fact and the fact that with a little better management that Magazine could have been kept going, encouraged me to hope for success.[3]

He also acknowledges that Miss Elliott (whose grandfather had founded the original *Southern Review* in 1828 and whose father had edited it for a time) has "helped much"; she appears as a reviewer of fiction and poetry in the third volume.

Trent was strongly supported by his powerful friends Wiggins and Gailor. Nevertheless, he felt increasingly uncomfortable at Sewanee and eventually decided he had to leave. Trent was against the system of

3. Franklin T. Walker, "W. P. Trent: A Critical Biography" (Ph.D. diss., Peabody College, Nashville, Tenn., 1943), 160.

student boardinghouses, presided over by matrons—ladies who, as he saw it, reinforced social and other prejudices; he advocated dormitories as more democratic and as improving school spirit. This proposal would have left the matrons (mostly Confederate and clerical widows) unemployed, and caused much outrage. Trent lost; the matron system remained, and was important in the Sewanee tradition of emphasis on manners, dress, and the social graces. Trent felt that many of his neighbors disliked him and regarded him as a traitor; he knew that each year a minority of the trustees denounced him as a dangerous religious and political heretic. He left Sewanee in 1900 to accept a professorship at Columbia, and is remembered there by a chair named in his honor.

When Trent resigned in 1900, Vice-Chancellor Wiggins stated to the trustees,

> To Dr. Trent more than to any other man, the University owes its reputation in literary studies. He made his school of English the first among the Southern institutions of higher learning. As editor of the *Sewanee Review,* and as author of the Life of William Gilmore Simms, . . . and other publications, and as a frequent contributor to the leading journals and magazines, Dr. Trent has spread abroad the fame of the University and has also been a great stimulus to literary activity on the part of his colleagues.[4]

In his later years Trent mellowed and became more sympathetic to the Old South and to the Episcopal Church. In 1935, he wrote to his old friend Thomas Gailor, then Bishop of Tennessee, who confirmed him at last, two years later, "When, in the fullness of time, an autopsy is made of this old body, it will be found that, like Bloody Mary, there is a single word engraved upon my heart. That word is not Calais, but Sewanee."

John Bell Henneman, who had been a classmate of Trent at the University of Virginia, came to Sewanee in 1900 to succeed him in the editorship and the chair of English. After Henneman's death in 1908,

---

4. Ibid., 229–30.

John McBryde was editor until 1919, when George Herbert Clarke, who had a considerable reputation as poet and anthologist, took over and began publishing a small amount of poetry in each issue. In 1926 William Skinkle Knickerbocker, who had taken his Ph.D. under Trent at Columbia, became editor and remained until 1942. Knickerbocker was opposed to the Agrarians and published little writing by any of the Fugitives, though he later claimed to have fostered both groups.

W. B. C. Watkins, a former Rhodes Scholar who was a promising young teacher at Princeton, was brought to Sewanee to edit the *Sewanee Review* in 1943. He found the constant rain and fog depressing, had a nervous breakdown, and left in a few months. (His name never appeared on the masthead.) His most notable book before his Sewanee debacle was *Perilous Balance,* a psychological study of Swift, Johnson, and Sterne; later, he had a distinguished career as critic and teacher.

After Knickerbocker's departure in 1942, the story of the *Sewanee Review* merges with that of Sewanee's other main source of literary connections, and we will return to it later. This other source of literary associations is simply Sewanee's location and topography: it is not only a most attractive place, but is close to Monteagle, whose Assembly (originally called the Sunday School Assembly, or Assembly Grounds) has been famous throughout this part of the South since the 1880s as a summer resort, and not far from Nashville, where the Fugitives and Agrarians were the center of a literary revival in the 1920s and 1930s. Andrew Lytle's family had owned a log cabin in the Assembly since 1907, and Andrew's friends from Vanderbilt—Allen Tate, Robert Penn Warren, Brainard Cheney, and others—visited him there and became interested in Sewanee. Cottages in the Assembly were cheap in winter, and the Tates came for two winters, as well as several summers; Robert Lowell and Jean Stafford also came, and Peter Taylor, whose family owned a cottage. The *Sewanee Review* was clearly in decline when Knickerbocker left in 1942; one critic called it "a haphazard receptacle for second-rate literary exercises." Lytle and Tate were concerned as they watched (from Monteagle much of the time), because they hoped to have the *Sewanee* carry on the role of the newly defunct *Southern Review.* After Knickerbocker finally left, Lytle reluctantly agreed during the next two years to serve as managing editor and do most of the editing, with much help from Tate. From 1943 on fiction was published in each issue, and the amount of space given to poetry was much increased; the quality of the criticism and its contemporary relevance were much improved.

The transformation was completed when Allen Tate took over in 1944. He had refused to accept the editorship until he was assured of money to pay contributors, considering this essential because it is a basic distinction between academic journals and magazines employing professional writers. He had the format completely redesigned, introduced prize competitions, and eventually quadrupled the circulation. He enlisted some of the best poets, critics, and fiction writers in the United States and England as contributors, and so brought the magazine into the first rank.[5] But we must leave the story of the *Review* after Tate's resignation in 1945 for the next essay.

From the beginning to 1909, the University's long vacation was in the winter, from November to February, and most of the early houses were not meant for winter habitation. Summer was the height of the social season. "The Gay Nineties were the heyday of the Summer Girl at Sewanee. She arrived for the 4th of July Hop and remained for Commencement in August. . . . Old Forensic could have told many tales of beaux and belles, of Red Ribbon Germans, and Snake and Fox Head Dances." Sewanee has always been a summer resort as well as a university town, and it retains something of the casual sociability of such places.

The University of the South has been well described as "one of the Utopian educational projects of nineteenth-century America"—though it must be immediately added that Episcopal respectability precluded any such radical notions as free love or communal property, as in such

---

5. Ann Waldron's *Close Connections: Caroline Gordon and the Southern Renaissance* (New York: G. P. Putnam's Sons, 1987) is a perceptive and entertaining treatment not only of Caroline Gordon and Allen Tate but also of Robert Lowell, Peter Taylor, Andrew Lytle, Ford Madox Ford, and many others. The picture of Tate given by Walter Sullivan in his *Allen Tate: A Recollection* (Baton Rouge: Louisiana State University Press, 1988), stressing his sexual conduct and his frailties in old age, seems to me to be a distorted one. Tate's "lightning kindness" and generosities, his disinterested helpfulness to aspiring writers, his gift for friendship, his sense of responsibility as man of letters—these qualities praised by so many people in their tributes are in Sullivan's account of Tate's late years in Sewanee made to seem self-serving, malicious, or manipulative.

other Utopian communities as Brook Farm, New Harmony, or Oneida. (At Sewanee, according to an early commentator, "people of eminent respectability live together in cheerful poverty.") The founders in 1858 presumably had Wordsworthian notions of the spiritually improving and other beneficial effects of unspoiled Nature on growing youth and the desirability of keeping them isolated, away from the corruptions and temptations of cities. This line of thought has always struck me as implausible, but Sewanee never fails to impress residents and visitors with its unspoiled natural beauty, together with its isolation; it is not only a towered city set within a wood, but a City on a Hill in both the literal and symbolic sense. Its domain is owned by the church and therefore inevitably perceived as somehow sanctified, kept unspotted from the world.

This perception tends to become embodied in the literary myth of pastoral or the biblical myth of Eden. William Alexander Percy, who came to Sewanee as a student in 1900, described it memorably in terms of the classical pastoral:

> The college has about three hundred young men or inmates, or students as they are sometimes called, and besides, quite a number of old ladies, who always were old and ladies, and who never die. It's a long way away, even from Chattanooga, in the middle of woods, on top of a bastion of mountains crenelated with blue coves. It is so beautiful that people who have once been there always, one way or another, come back. For such as can detect apple green in an evening sky, it is Arcadia—not the one that never used to be, but the one that many people always live in; only this one can be shared. . . .
>
> When the Arcadians are fools, as they sometimes are, you do not deplore their stupidity, and when they are brilliant you do not resent their intellectuality. The reason is, their manners—the kind not learned or instilled but happening, the core being sweet—are far realer than their other qualities. . . . What Pan and Dionysos and the old ladies dower them with is supplemented by an influence which must appear to the uninitiated incompatible . . . the Arcadians at seven each morning are driven, not without maledictions, to divine service.[6]

6. William Alexander Percy, *Lanterns on the Levee: Recollections of a Planter's Son* (Baton Rouge: Louisiana State University Press, 1989 [originally 1941]), 96, 101.

Percy may be forgiven for some sentimentalizing when we remember that he is writing with open nostalgia of a time some forty years in the past, looking back to an imaginary Eden of his youth. His English teacher was J. B. Henneman, who (as we have seen) came to Sewanee to succeed Trent in 1900. When Henneman died in 1908, Percy was brought back to Sewanee to take his place (in teaching only, not the editing) for six months. William Alexander Percy's nephew, the novelist Walker Percy, maintained the Sewanee connection; he was a frequent visitor to Sewanee (staying in the Percy family house, "Brinkwood," and often accompanied by his friend, Shelby Foote, later to gain fame as novelist and historian of the Civil War) and a contributor to and for many years an advisory editor of the *Sewanee Review.* When Walker Percy was obliged to give up his medical career in 1942 after contracting tuberculosis, he came to Sewanee to try writing; his first novel, still unpublished, was a kind of roman à clef about Sewanee and its inhabitants.

To look for a moment at the other—realistic—side of pastoral, we remember that the pastoral faun was in real life simply a goat, with all its gross and unpleasant connotations. The train that came up from Cowan once a day was called the Mountain Goat, and so was the student humor magazine, which expressed the goatish side of the Arcadians. And, as Sewanee's theologians—who have tended toward the Augustinian—would be the first to point out, there are in reality no unfallen Edens: the Serpent has been everywhere, and there is a worm in every apple. The Anglo-Catholic St. Andrew's (now St. Andrew's-Sewanee) was notoriously High (though the hair preserved as sacred relic of St. Charles the Martyr seems to have been only legendary) and Augustinian.

Sewanee can seem like an earthly paradise: its flowers and trees, especially in spring and fall, vistas of gentle mountains, picturesque coves, lush farmlands below, are beautiful, varied, and kept unspoiled. The inhabitants, too, give the impression of a kind of innocence: the genteel poverty tinged with Episcopal piety in which most of them traditionally lived, combined with a high degree of social sophistication and cultural cosmopolitanism—for example, the close links with Oxford maintained from the beginning, and a tendency to unbridled

Anglophilia. (At one time Sewanee's chapter of the English-Speaking Union was surpassed in size only by Boston's.) But there is, of course, always a dark underside, a serpent in the Garden, a worm in the apple.

This aspect is described most movingly in *Ely: An Autobiography*, by Ely Green.[7] Green, child of a black servant and a white son (he never knew which of two brothers) of one of Sewanee's most respectable families, wrote late in life a wonderfully vivid and detailed account of his early years. He was born in 1893 and left Sewanee in 1912; thus, ironically enough, his account covers the same period so idyllically described by William Alexander Percy. But Green's account is no bitter diatribe; it is all the more heart-rending because he was treated with respect and love by most white people in Sewanee, and thus came late to awareness of his divided situation. He was baptized by the university chaplain, with Bishop Gailor as his godfather. When he and other blacks were invited to come in and watch a university dance, "This was the first time I realized something about me that was not fair—white people just let a Negro go so far and no farther, though we were a part of them and they were a part of us. Why were we at a handicap? No answer. I had worn out the patience out of everybody asking questions" (78). His white paternal grandfather had been a Confederate officer; his black maternal grandfather was Ned Green, swill hauler and privy cleaner, one of the most vivid characters in *Ely*. Ely, who had been brought up mainly in, or close to, the white world, was fascinated by his black grandfather's independence and country knowledge, and by his curious religious attitude. "I believe in the Communion of Saints but not the Resurrection," Ned mumbles, and again, "Confound it, if I could get this Resurrection in my head it might be better. . . . God-ding the Communion of Saints" (98, 116). Again, "I just can't get it. I don't say there is not a God, but I don't get this Resurrection. Father Eastern and Father Clabern talks to me. I just can't get it. I know you are a Christian. You have to be the way these niggers have treated you because a white man is your daddy. And it's not your fault. Don't let them kick you around anymore,

7. Ely Green, *Ely: An Autobiography* (Athens: University of Georgia Press, 1990). Originally published in 1966 by the Seabury Press.

Christian or no Christian. I want you to be a man among men like me. Don't have no boss. Make your own job" (173). But the washfoot Baptist parson takes all he can get of Ned's provisions, and Ely accepts Father Eastern's explanation of why the emotional religions in the valley are dangerous (86–89). As Bertram Wyatt-Brown well says in his foreword to the 1990 paperback edition, "Along with the works of those notables who wrote for the *Sewanee Review,* Ely Green's memoir belongs in the southern literary canon and merits a wide and enduring readership."

Sewanee as Arcadia or as unfallen Eden (or Dantean Earthly Paradise) is highly vulnerable to parody, but both myths are persistent and significant. The Edenic version was perhaps best rendered (symbolically, not explicitly) by James Agee, who was a student at St. Andrew's school from 1919 to 1923 and much later embodied his crucial religious experience in a short novel, *The Morning Watch* (1950). The novel describes the ten-year-old protagonist's effort to pray and to keep the morning watch on the night before Good Friday. After much conscientious self-torment and self-reproach he and his friends give up the attempt and go swimming, reveling in the beauty of the natural world; after almost drowning himself, the boy returns to the world in a pagan resurrection and kills a snake, for which he reproaches himself; but at the end he accepts death and resurrection—exemplified in the snake and a locust that he finds, both having discarded their skins or shells—as part of nature. His Eden, then, is natural, with death as part of the natural cycle, not a result of original sin.

The year before his death, Agee described to Father Flye his idea for a scene for *Candide* (which Lillian Hellman and Leonard Bernstein were working on): "I will write of Eldorado, the Earthly Paradise . . . the celebration of a birth; the intent for divorce and re-marriage; and the intent to die."[8] Candide asks, after finding that euthanasia is permitted, " 'So, you all believe in a life after death?' The king gently shrugs: 'It is one of the few questions on which we differ among ourselves.' " The inhabitants of this ideal community have never heard of Christianity.

8. James Agee, *Letters of James Agee to Father Flye* (Boston: Houghton, Mifflin, 1971 [originally 1962]), 216–17.

The dedication of the James Agee Memorial Library at St. Andrew's in October 1972 is commemorated in *Remembering James Agee* (1974), edited by David Madden. David McDowell, who was a senior at St. Andrew's in 1936 when Agee returned there for a long visit with Father Flye, and later became Agee's biographer (and editor and publisher of *A Death in the Family*), arranged the celebration, attended by novelists, critics, scholars, clergymen, and students. *Remembering* contains essays by friends and associates of Agee from his Harvard days through his time at *Fortune* and *Time* and his work as a writer for and critic of films.

When he retired from the University of Minnesota in 1968, Allen Tate returned to Sewanee to live. He continued to teach at Sewanee from time to time, and always to offer help to promising writers and to the *Sewanee Review*. In 1974 there was a gratifying celebration in Sewanee of Tate's seventy-fifth birthday: Louis Rubin, Denis Donoghue, Cleanth Brooks, and Walter Sullivan gave papers, and guests came from far and near. For reasons of health, Tate had to move to Nashville in 1976, and died there in 1979; he is buried in Sewanee. The Sewanee literary tradition owes more to Tate than anyone else, because of his wide acquaintance in the literary world, the special warmth and respect he inspired in other writers, and his integrity and devotion to literature. Much is owed to Trent and succeeding editors, and especially to Andrew Lytle. But Tate's role in shaping the magazine for the second half of its century was preeminent and decisive.

The Aiken Taylor awards (endowed by Conrad Aiken's younger brother) have been since 1987 an important part of Sewanee's tradition of honoring poetry: Howard Nemerov, Richard Wilbur, Anthony Hecht, W. S. Merwin, J. F. Nims, Gwendolyn Brooks, George Starbuck, and Wendell Berry have been the recipients so far.

The Sewanee Writers' Conference held its first session in the summer of 1990, subsidized by Tennessee Williams's joint legacy to Sewanee and Harvard (the Sewanee portion a memorial to his grandfather, Fr. Walter E. Dakin, who was a Sewanee alumnus of 1895). The first session was a great success, with Howard Nemerov, Mona Van Duyn, Tim O'Brien, and Robert Stone among the faculty members, and an enthusiastic group of students; the subsequent ones have shown further growth in size and prestige. Appropriately to the theatrical benefactor, recent ones have featured such playwrights as Arthur Miller and Horton Foote. The conference is directed by Wyatt Prunty, who was brought back to the university as Carlton Professor and the first permanent and official teacher of writing. Prunty is the best-known poet and critic to have graduated from Sewanee, with the possible exception of Richard Tillinghast, who wrote *Sewanee in Ruins* during his tenure as Brown Foundation fellow in 1981. (The university has used Brown Foundation fellowships to bring such younger writers as Kent Nelson, Alan Cheuse, Mark Richard, and Elizabeth Dewberry Vaughn to Sewanee, as well as Tate, Lytle, and Prunty.)

The latest development is the Sewanee Young Writers' Conference, which began in the summer of 1994. It is open to promising writers of high school age from anywhere in the United States. Horton Foote, Ellen Douglas, Andrew Hudgins, and Alice McDermott will participate in this as well as the senior conference in 1995, and the Young Writers have their own faculty in addition.

Let me recapitulate some of the main themes I have been trying to suggest in this somewhat rambling discussion. Universities and colleges are often mythopoeic; bright college years are seen nostalgically as an age of innocence, before the Fall (for example, the Princeton of *This Side of Paradise,* the Oxford of *Brideshead Revisited).* This tendency is encouraged by the air of fantasy and unreality produced by incongruity between a university and its surroundings, as in Oxford, Princeton, and especially Sewanee, a medieval city in the backwoods. Myths of Sewanee inevitably portray it as the home of the Lost Cause, of retired Confederate generals and bishops, or their widows. But—with the single exception of Sarah Barnwell Elliott—there were no writers until in 1892 Trent started the *Sewanee Review* and with it the Sewanee literary tradition. We have seen the pagan myth of Arcadia and the Romantic one of innocence and the lost childhood in William Alexander Percy; of expulsion from Eden and from belief in James Agee. Andrew Lytle's version of the Sewanee myth puts it in terms of the Fall into History; *The Velvet Horn's* Jungian patterns repeat and complicate Agee's in *The Morning Watch*—but both are deeply imbued with the symbolism of natural cycles and of the Fall in all its richly ambiguous meanings. (Lytle discusses the myth explicitly in his recent book of essays, *From*

Eden to Babylon.) Historically, William Alexander Percy and Ely Green portray Sewanee in 1900–1909, James Agee St. Andrew's about 1920. Then the modern literary tradition really begins with Lytle and Tate and the transformed *Sewanee Review* of 1943–1945.

I have no wish to make inflated claims that the university has produced an extraordinary number of writers, or that Sewanee has been the specific setting for many poems or novels, or has a sacred spring that can be relied on to inspire visiting writers. Caroline Gordon's "Those Brilliant Leaves" may be the best story set in Sewanee-Monteagle except for Peter Taylor's "Heads of Houses." (The location in Taylor's stories and in his play *A Stand in the Mountains* is so generalized that it could extend from Beersheba Springs to Lookout Mountain, though clearly Sewanee-Monteagle is central, and always suggests the last stand of Southern society.) Taylor, long a frequent visitor and homeowner (and contributor to the *Review*), was (with his wife, the poet Eleanor Ross Taylor) a regular summer resident.

Aside from Andrew Lytle, who was first in his class at Sewanee Military Academy, George Garrett is, as far as I know, the only S.M.A. alumnus of literary note. In *Whistling in the Dark* (1992) he presents a vivid picture of S.M.A. during World War II. Poet, critic, novelist, he is a frequent visitor and friend of the *Review*. Lytle has never used Sewanee specifically as a setting in his fiction, as far as I am aware, but discusses it and Middle Tennessee in general in *A Wake for the Living* (1975) and *From Eden to Babylon* (1990).

I have stressed mythic themes partly in order to counteract the tendency, inevitable in discussing a subject like this one, to sound like the public relations office or the most sentimental of alumni. I have not attempted to define precisely either "Sewanee" or "writer," recognizing that in these formidably theoretical days to do so might require disproportionate time. But, though I haven't tried to be rigorous, either historically or critically, I have found in these notions about myth and about the central importance of the *Sewanee Review* a path through the tangles of history and anecdote that seemed worth exploring.

∽

CHAPTER 4

Reflections on the

Centennial of the

Sewanee Review

LIKE SO MANY THINGS since Caesar's Gaul, the role of the *Sewanee Review* in the "Southern Renascence" may be divided into three parts. The first consists of the period from the founding of the *Review* in 1892 through 1925. As we have seen in the preceding chapter, the *Sewanee* was intended to perform the Arnoldian function of producing the kind of intellectual milieu in which criticism and literature could flourish. Its contribution to the beginning of the Southern Renascence was chiefly to provide general intellectual stimulation and increased respect for literature.

When W. P. Trent, the founder, left for Columbia University in 1900, he was succeeded as editor of *Sewanee* by John Bell Henneman. Henneman was also an impressive teacher, described by his star pupil William Alexander Percy as "passionate, black-bearded, bespectacled, with . . . a capacity for furious moral tantrums." He edited the volume on *The Intellectual Life* in the thirteen-volume set *The South in the Building of the Nation*, once a feature of every well-appointed Southern library.

Based on a lecture read at the Sewanee Writers' Conference in July 1992 and published partly in the *South Carolina Review* for fall 1992 and partly in the *Sewanee Review* for the same date.

After his death in 1908, John M. McBryde became editor; when he resigned in 1919, after a difficult tenure complicated by the university's financial problems and the First World War, George Herbert Clarke, an Englishman educated in Canada, was brought in. He had a considerable reputation as poet and anthologist, and began the practice of publishing poetry in the magazine. He began boldly by publishing one of his own poems. Most of the poetry was, naturally, unremarkable; but in 1922 the first page of the first issue contained Ransom's "Winter Remembered" (as a regular Shakespearean sonnet rather than in its final form as five quatrains, but still a wonderful poem), and Clarke deserves credit for recognizing its quality and giving it due prominence. Clarke also published poems by Laura Riding Gottschalk, Robert Penn Warren, and Donald Davidson, essays by Davidson and Ransom, and another fine poem by Ransom, "The Dead Boy." He tried to raise money to establish an endowment for the magazine, but was unsuccessful. In 1925 he left to teach at Queen's University in Canada.

The second period coincides with the editorship of William Skinkle Knickerbocker, from 1926 to 1942. When Knickerbocker took over in 1926, there was an immediate sharp decline in the poetry: nothing more from the Nashville group, and a great deal by Knickerbocker, his family, and his friends. (But he did, mysteriously, print poems by Theodore Roethke twice, in 1932 and 1938.) Knickerbocker was a New Yorker who took his Ph.D. under Trent at Columbia, with a special interest in Victorian literature and education. He was a strong advocate of the New or Advancing South, and assumed the curious posture of opposing the Nashville Fugitive-Agrarians while simultaneously claiming credit for having fostered them and published a little of their early prose. In 1927 he did print an important essay by Allen Tate, "Poetry and the Absolute," and in the next year, as he never tired of reminding his readers, the piece by Ransom that became the lead essay in *I'll Take My Stand*. In 1934 he wrote, "The Agrarian movement was launched in these pages by Mr. John Crowe Ransom's now-famous essay, 'The South—Old or New,' which in the rephrased form of 'Reconstructed but Unregenerate' introduces . . . *I'll Take My Stand*." But the Agrarians, he continues with injured magnanimity, "having been adopted by the New York publication, *The American Review*, continue

their propaganda. . . . Doubtless they will again appear in the pages
of this Quarterly when occasion arises." While Knickerbocker liked
Ransom personally, he ridiculed and opposed the Agrarian principles
("Nashville Yeomanism") and called *God Without Thunder* "theological
homebrew" or "thunder without God." He engaged in public debates
with Ransom and Davidson before large audiences, but he did not
allow both sides of the debate to be adequately represented in the
magazine. Ransom writes to Tate in 1930, "Yes, Knickerbocker is my
opponent [in the forthcoming debate] and he came in the office here
Wednesday, after first asking if I had a gun. He is as cheery, friendly,
bright, and foolish as ever."[1] In 1937, Knickerbocker wrote, sounding
rather like Miss Piggy, *"Moi,* I am anathema to most of the Agrarians but,
in this forty-fifth year of *The Sewanee Review,* . . . I note that Mr. Ransom in person and in print has been one of my most indispensable
dons," and he expressed regret that Ransom was leaving Vanderbilt for
Kenyon.

   The long and painful process of Knickerbocker's leaving Sewanee
may be seen in the Lytle-Tate letters; the magazine was clearly in
decline (Tate called it "a graveyard for second-rate professors"[2]), and
the vice-chancellor clearly wanted to get rid of Knickerbocker, but to
allow him to keep his dignity and resign rather than be fired. Lytle
calls him "plainly unbalanced and not responsible for his speech and
acts." In 1941 Ransom commented on Knickerbocker's "crazy spell":
"He reviewed Burke's book and mine together after his wildest manner,
then started in writing a letter a day to Burke, and sending me the
carbon copy" *(Letters,* 286). When he finally left in 1942 he went to
New England, a region presumably more congenial, though he had
praised the South and Sewanee fulsomely in his last few editorials (Tate
had remarked earlier that he was inclined to "fawning"), claiming credit
once more for fostering the Fugitives: "No longer is it necessary for me
to speak of them with a sense of vox clamantis in deserto."

   1. Thomas D. Young and George Core, eds., *Selected Letters of John Crowe Ransom*
(Baton Rouge: Louisiana State University Press, 1985), 202.
   2. Thomas D. Young and Elizabeth Sarcone, eds., *The Lytle-Tate Letters: The Correspondence of Andrew Lytle and Allen Tate* (Jackson: University Press of Mississippi, 1987), 186.

The *Sewanee,* then, in this second period was important to the Nashville group mainly as a goad, gadfly, or thorn in the flesh; and it showed no awareness of literary developments elsewhere in the South.

The final period, however, extending from 1942 to the present, or whenever one chooses to say the Southern Renascence ended, is very different. Both Andrew Lytle and Allen Tate were concerned in 1942 to have the *Sewanee* carry on the role of the newly defunct *Southern Review,* and after Knickerbocker finally left, Lytle reluctantly agreed during the next two years to serve as managing editor and do most of the editing, with much help from Tate. From 1943 on fiction was published in each issue, and the amount of space given to poetry was much increased; the quality of the criticism and its contemporary relevance were much improved.

The transformation was completed when Tate took over in 1944. He had refused to accept the editorship until he was assured of money to pay contributors, considering this essential because it is a basic distinction between academic journals and magazines employing professional writers. He had the format of the magazine completely redesigned, introduced prize competitions, and eventually quadrupled the circulation. The South was very well represented, although the emphasis was not exclusively or even primarily regional, but international: the magazine undertook to present a selection of the best criticism, fiction, and poetry being produced in the United States, secondarily in England, and (to a limited extent) Canada, Ireland, and sometimes France and Italy.

In his short editorship Tate brought the magazine into the first rank, with status at least equal to that of the *Kenyon* and *Partisan* reviews. (I must remark in passing on the astonishing formative genius exhibited by Tate in the early 1940s: first he established the program in the Creative Arts at Princeton, serving as first resident poet and bringing in R. P. Blackmur as his assistant; then he became, not technically but effectively, the first Consultant in Poetry at the Library of Congress; and then he became editor of the *Sewanee.* In each case he defined and shaped the position, pioneering in a new situation; and in each case the mold that he formed has lasted for a long time. In the same period, he was writing some of his finest poetry and criticism.)

Speaking very broadly, all succeeding editors have maintained the same basic editorial policy established by Tate and Lytle. John Palmer, who was editor from 1946 to 1952, had been managing editor of the *Southern Review,* and perhaps because of this experience somewhat increased the Southern emphasis, publishing, for example, Katherine Anne Porter, Eudora Welty, Robert Penn Warren, even William Faulkner, and early work of Flannery O'Connor. Palmer invited Tate and Warren to edit a special issue in 1948 in honor of Ransom's sixtieth birthday. When he was called back into the navy because of the Korean War, Palmer attempted briefly to edit the *Review* from London, where he was Assistant Naval Attaché, but then found it necessary to resign. When the job was offered to me, I took it, though it was an awkward time (I was on leave from Vanderbilt, working intensively on an eighteenth-century project), because I admired the *Review* so much and my wife and I had fallen in love with Sewanee as a place after Palmer had introduced us to it.

In my inaugural editorial in *Sewanee,* I stated that I intended to preserve the character of the magazine as Tate and Palmer had formed it. "Insofar as they had any explicit policy (beyond that of presenting the best poetry, fiction, and criticism available), it was evidently that suggested by the history and provenance of the magazine. . . . It has never stood for a crude regionalism; but, representing and interpreting the traditional South, it has also represented an international community of letters."

I enlisted Allen Tate and Andrew Lytle as advisory editors, with Francis Fergusson to counterbalance these Southerners, and we were enabled by the bounty of the Rockefeller Foundation to give fellowships to some twenty younger writers. Though by no means all of these were Southern, many were, among them James Dickey, Madison Jones, George Garrett, and Louis Rubin—all of whom were also regular contributors to the magazine. Of course, I took special pleasure in publishing Tate, Warren, Ransom, Walker Percy, Flannery O'Connor, and other major Southern writers. But in the special issue in 1958 celebrating the centennial of the university's founding, the two literary essays were by Lionel Trilling and Philip Wheelwright, who were emphatically not Southerners. A special issue for Allen Tate's sixtieth birthday in

1959 brought together essays, poems, and tributes by many of his old friends and colleagues, Southern and other. (The list is worth giving: R. P. Blackmur, Malcolm Cowley, Donald Davidson, T. S. Eliot, Francis Fergusson, Anthony Hecht, Robert Lowell, Andrew Lytle, Jacques and Raissa Maritain, Arthur Mizener, Howard Nemerov, Katherine Anne Porter, John Crowe Ransom, Sir Herbert Read, Mark Van Doren, Eliseo Vivas, John Hall Wheelock, and Reed Whittemore.)

After I resigned in 1961, Lytle took over; because of his long career as a teacher of writers of fiction, the magazine's emphasis on fiction, especially by younger Southern writers, naturally increased. But when Eliot died in 1965, Lytle invited Tate to edit a special Eliot issue that was also published as a book in 1966 and was highly acclaimed. The basic pattern of the magazine remained unchanged during Lytle's tenure, as it did when George Core took over in 1973 and restated it in his inaugural editorial in 1974. Though he suggested there that he expected to decrease the Southern emphasis, he appointed Walker Percy as an advisory editor (replaced by Elizabeth Spencer in 1990) and when Ransom died in 1974, devoted an issue to his life and work. Core has now surpassed Knickerbocker's record to become the longest-serving editor in *Sewanee's* history. He did eventually carry out his intention to restore the balance by giving more attention to British writers and publishing special issues on Commonwealth writers and on Ireland.

Core has had the primary responsibility for the Aiken Taylor award for poetry given each year since 1987 by the *Sewanee Review* and the University of the South. The award was established by a bequest from Dr. K. P. A. Taylor, a younger brother of the poet Conrad Aiken; the prize is substantial (ten thousand dollars), and the occasion is celebrated by appropriate festivities and gatherings. Core has also obtained endowments to establish annual prizes for the best story and best essay published in the magazine, and has generously honored his two immediate predecessors, Lytle and Spears, by naming the prizes for them. (A third prize, for reviewing, has just been established and named for Robert B. Heilman.) The *Review* and the university honored Andrew Lytle on his eightieth birthday in 1982 and again on his ninetieth.

To sum up, the *Sewanee Review* was obviously not as important in the early Southern Renascence as *The Fugitive,* the New Orleans *Double*

Dealer, the *Southern Review* 1935–1942, or the *Kenyon Review* from 1939 on. While it certainly helped to raise intellectual standards in the South and to encourage that free play of ideas that Trent had found so lacking in Simms's day and his own, its most important function came late, from 1942 on, in confirming and validating the achievement of the major Southern writers and in encouraging new ones—for example, in publishing Cowley's essay that marked the beginning of Faulkner's rise to international fame and in publishing and awarding fellowships to younger Southern writers. But *Sewanee* was able to do this precisely because it was not primarily regional, but a part of a Republic of Letters that transcended not only the regional but the national, and was able therefore to put Southern writers in this international context. The chief service of the *Sewanee Review* to Southern writers in the whole period since 1942 has been to give them international recognition by publishing them in the best possible company, regardless of regional or national origin, and to subject them to the best available critical interpretation and evaluation.

As we look back in 1992 at the history of the magazine, the first remarkable thing to notice is the simple fact of survival for one hundred years: it is indeed America's oldest literary quarterly to be continuously published under the same name. The founders of the University of the South envisioned a literary magazine from the beginning, but it was the initiative, enterprise, and energy of W. P. Trent that made it happen. He could not have done so, however, without the encouragement and help of the highest officials of the university: the Rev. Telfair Hodgson, vice-chancellor and dean of the School of Theology, acted as managing editor for the first year; Benjamin Wiggins, professor of Greek and later vice-chancellor, took over the business responsibilities and was a strong supporter, as was Thomas Gailor, chaplain and later vice-chancellor and then Bishop of Tennessee. Though Trent was an iconoclastic, outspoken, sometimes abrasive and difficult young man, these officials not only tolerated but highly valued him and worked with him enthusiastically on the magazine. The university administrators are remarkable in thus having recognized from the beginning what an important asset the *Review* is and in never wavering in their commitment to support it. (I refrain from giving examples of other universities that have killed and then attempted to resurrect or transfigure their quarterlies, often several times.)

It might be objected that the *Sewanee Review* of 1942 was so different from that of 1944 that it was no longer the same magazine. Certainly the change was fundamental, but not so radical as to mean a total shift of identity. There were many elements of continuity: in the first place, a good many contributors continued on both sides of the change, such as Austin Warren, Arthur Mizener, Mark Schorer, Eliseo Vivas, Charles Harrison, and other first-rate academic critics. In the second place, the same apparent design was continued: a review primarily critical, consisting of essays and book reviews, dignified and responsible in attitude, and, until 1943, a little poetry. The change consisted in boosting the quantity and quality of the poetry enormously, adding first-rate fiction, and changing the attitude of the criticism from academic-historical to vital concern with the present as well as the past. On both sides of the divide, the magazine kept its readers aware of the perspectives of history, philosophy, and religion, while remaining primarily literary.

But the essence of the new pattern established by Lytle and Tate seems to me to have consisted of two things (in addition to having better editors to begin with). First, the magazine was made professional by paying contributors and by making its format more attractive and thus, with better advertising and distribution, expanding its circulation. This made it competitive both in obtaining manuscripts and in obtaining readers, rather than passive and unrelated to the marketplace as strictly academic periodicals are. Tate, who had been a regional editor of *Hound and Horn* and the most important adviser to Brooks and Warren at the *Southern Review* and to Ransom at the *Kenyon Review,* and thus "probably the most important force in shaping the history of the critical review in the United States,"[3] would not take the editorship of *Sewanee* until money to pay contributors was assured. There is a certain element of make-believe in the financial aspect—such magazines are not really commercial, always requiring a substantial subsidy, and the payments to contributors are ridiculously far from being enough to live

3. G. A. M. Janssens, *The American Literary Review: A Critical History 1920–1950* (The Hague and Paris: Mouton, 1968), 208.

on; but experience has shown that this serious make-believe makes a tremendous difference in the nature of the magazine. Tate knew this, and demonstrated it in his brief but decisive editorship.

Second, both fiction and poetry were published, and the quality as well as quantity of both were greatly increased. The inclusion of "creative" writing of the highest quality, some of it by well-known writers and some by new and promising ones, had been an essential feature of the best literary reviews since the *Dial* began in 1920 and the *Criterion* in 1922.

It seems to me that, insofar as there is any secret formula in the composition of an excellent literary quarterly, it is the presence of both these ingredients and their mutual interaction. The poetry and fiction keep the critics aware of the living presence of literature here and now and restrain any tendency to excessive abstraction and aridity; the critical essays and reviews keep the poets and fiction writers from any tendency to self-indulgence and self-absorption. There is inevitably a tension between the two activities and attitudes, but it can be a fruitful and mutually beneficial one.

Similarly, it is important to have some of the writing in both kinds transcend not only regional but national borders, so that both writers and readers are aware of an international community of letters. The *Sewanee Review* in its earlier history always had some British and Canadian contributors, and the pattern since 1944 has greatly increased this emphasis, including some attention even to French and Italian writing.

I don't mean to suggest that *Sewanee* is the only magazine to keep to this basic pattern, but it has maintained it longer than any other; each editor succeeding Tate has professed his allegiance to it on taking office, not merely out of piety but because of the conviction that it works. The *Sewanee* has thus become an institution, with a revolution (or perhaps renascence) almost exactly in the middle of its hundred-year history. The great benefits of being an institution are stability and responsibility; the dangers are dullness and complacency. An institution, being itself a part of history, is not likely to neglect the past; it is more likely to fail in being sufficiently aware of the present and in ability to change in response to challenges.

I should argue that the maintenance of this relation between criticism and creative writing is especially important at present, when there are strong pressures in the universities to separate them. When criticism becomes dominated by "theory," explicitly denying any concern with creative writing or with the evaluation of contemporary writing, and on the other hand creative writing, vulgarly called "CW," becomes an enormous industry on its own, appealing to students by rigorously avoiding elitism, the situation is very unhealthy. The pattern of a critical quarterly like the *Sewanee* seems to me to be, in these times, a paradigm of the proper relations between the two: criticism informed by an awareness of the problems of the contemporary poet or fiction writer, and poetry and fiction informed by an awareness of the perspectives and standards of the best criticism.

As T. S. Eliot remarked as long ago as 1923, Matthew Arnold distinguished far too bluntly between criticism and creation: "He overlooks the capital importance of criticism in the work of creation itself." "The critical activity finds its highest, its true fulfilment in a kind of union with creation in the labour of the artist." The writer needs himself to be a good critic and he needs an audience that is critically aware. And the critic needs to be able to take the writer's point of view. Eliot himself showed how important he considered keeping the two together by devoting seventeen years of his time to editing the *Criterion,* which has remained in many respects a model for subsequent literary magazines.

If this argument seems old hat or to be taken for granted or obvious, let me cite an example of a very different and apparently popular attitude. Here is an essay by Ron Tanner in the *Associated Writing Programs Chronicle* for March/April 1991. (*Associated Writing Programs Chronicle* now represents more than two hundred writing programs and claims twelve thousand readers; I know nothing about Tanner and his other writings, if any.) Tanner says,

> The most common criticism of creative writing is that it grants authority to the student-as-subject rather than to the subject (literature) itself. . . . Creative writing appears to be anti-traditionalist because it presumes . . . to produce artists. Indeed . . . academic creative writing is unabashedly

egalitarian, operating on the assumption that nearly anyone, with practice and earnest application, can learn to write reasonably well. . . .
This is why although no one teaching creative writing claims that these
students will become financial or critical successes as a result of their
schooling, no one is discounting the possibility either. To the staunch
traditionalist such democratic optimism is anathema, for it flies in the
face of a still-cherished notion of Art as something created by a gifted
few for a privileged, i.e. "educated," audience.

Creative Writing is thus "potentially anarchic." During the last thirty
years the two areas of study that have become the financial mainstays
of English departments are creative writing and composition, and their
growth represents, according to Tanner, "not the decadence, more
specifically called the 'lowering of standards,' of English studies but
its restructuring to accommodate . . . students who, for a number of
cultural and social reasons, have greater need for composition than
their predecessors and who, because they are uninhibited by traditional
constraints or standards, demand the opportunity to express themselves 'creatively.'" Tanner concludes that academic creative writing is a
"symptom of health, of growth, and possibly of changes that were fore-
shadowed in the last century, when education and cheap books became
more accessible to most Americans and social mobility more possible";
therefore writers "shouldn't let themselves be bullied into doing things,
such as writing 'critical' papers, that don't in some constructive way
help their teaching and understanding of Creative Writing."

This is a wonderfully simplistic exposition of the situation from the
CW point of view. It is the Politically Correct anti-elitist argument in
its most extreme form: concern with quality is elitist, anyone can write,
pop art is just as good as high or mandarin. A. Walton Litz, when
he accepted the temporary position of head of the creative writing
program at Princeton, remarked that most English departments now
"have become the last repository for bad philosophy, bad sociology,
bad history," and that "Creative Writing programs of the next twenty
years will be like monasteries in the Middle Ages: they're going to be the
places where literature is actually enjoyed and taught." But if the people
in charge of these programs believe arguments like Tanner's, then CW
programs will have an opposite effect from what Litz predicted.

My pragmatic suggestion is that segregation of CW programs from the critical and historical study of literature is a fundamental mistake; integration is stimulating and invigorating for both sides. (I am, of course, not attempting to pontificate about how English departments and writing programs should be related administratively; I am arguing only that matters should be arranged so that the two activities are not kept completely apart.)

A critical quarterly like the *Sewanee,* then, is a perpetual demonstration of the possibility and importance of bringing the critical and creative activities together. Since the *Sewanee* is now, in its hundredth year, most impressively an institution surviving through a long vista of time, it also demonstrates the importance of keeping the past alive in the present, of preserving the sense of the past while remaining alert and receptive to the current situation in the arts.

CHAPTER 5

~

James

Dickey's

Poetry

LET ME ENTER the biographical mode, very briefly, to tell what I can remember about my first acquaintance with James Dickey. After four years in the military, I returned from France and was discharged in April of 1946. I had just turned thirty. An interview at Vanderbilt led me to accept a job there beginning in September, and I came to Nashville early in June to work desperately in the library, making up for the four lost years. (My life would have been very different if I had accepted instead the job I was offered at Princeton, where I had taken my Ph.D. before the war.)

Dickey arrived at Vanderbilt at about the same time, aged twenty-three. He has told the story of how his first Freshman English teacher, William Hunter, encouraged him and of how his second (Vanderbilt was on the quarter system), my wife Betty, introduced him to me. I might fill in the picture by adding some details from behind the scenes. When Betty started to correct and grade her first batch of themes from that class—she had assigned "Head by Scopas," by Edward Donaghue, in *Understanding Fiction*—she brought me one that she said

Read at the celebration of Dickey's seventieth birthday and twenty-fifth year of teaching at the University of South Carolina in September 1993.

68

she was troubled about: it was so much better written and so much more sophisticated than the others that she wondered if it could have been copied. I read it and assured her that there was no reason to suspect plagiarism: there were a few small flaws that would mark it as nonprofessional, but most importantly, it was a far better essay than anything the student could have found in print. A most extraordinary student, I said, and I'd like to meet him. So Betty introduced us, and Dickey took several of my classes.

In contrast to the boldness and authority of his writing, Dickey in person was very unassuming and mild. In class his behavior was impeccable: he was quiet, but willing to talk when called on or when comments were appropriate. He was considerate of other students and never intimidated or embarrassed them by showing off his obviously superior abilities. Our significant discussions took place, however, not in class but at odd times in my office, usually with Dickey standing or leaning in the door. (I always invited him to sit down, but he seemed more comfortable standing, I suppose through diffidence and fear of imposing.) He would, however, sit down when he brought me his poems to read.

As I look back on it, the divergence between us in temperament and interests when we began these discussions was so extreme as to seem almost comic. There were basic similarities: we had both spent almost four years in the army and were eager to leave all that behind and get on with careers in teaching and writing; we were both Southerners, lawyers' sons, passionately concerned with poetry. But I had been stationed most recently in Casablanca and Paris, where I had written Air Force history and had some acquaintance with French intellectual life; he had been flying night fighters in the Pacific, most recently from Okinawa with its particular horrors of kamikazes and mass suicides. I was working intensively on poets who were concerned mainly with the public world of reasonable discourse, civic responsibility, satire, light verse, and comedy in a social context, with technique and craftsmanship and refinement in art. Dryden, Pope, Prior, and Auden were my main focus in poetry. Dickey, in contrast, was immersed in anthropological and mythological reading; rituals of initiation, rites de passage, myths of the hero, confrontation with fear and violent death were not mere academic terms but described experiences he had been through. He was strongly influenced by surrealist and apocalyptic poetry and by the literature of vision and revelation. He liked George Barker, Kenneth Patchen, Dylan Thomas; Hart Crane especially, and most especially Theodore Roethke. In his own poetry he was trying to make sense of his recent experience and encompass its shocking juxtapositions: a middle-class suburban background in Atlanta followed by an abortive college year as a track and football jock at Clemson, and then a rapid transition to exotic and beautiful Pacific islands filled with violence, brutality, and sudden death.

Dickey at this stage was an extremely difficult and often obscure poet, and I take some satisfaction in the fact that I was able to recognize the real thing even when it appeared in a form not very congenial to me. I didn't try to change him, but I did suggest to him that some consideration should be given to the reader and that form as well as vision was important. He even went so far as to write some heroic couplets for me, though neither of us wanted him to try to become Alexander Pope. He did not convert me to admiration of George Barker or Kenneth Patchen, though I remember that we agreed about Randall Jarrell, about whom we both had mixed feelings, and about Dylan Thomas and many others.

Dickey published some poems in *The Gadfly,* the Vanderbilt student literary magazine, as early as 1947; but his first poem in a major quarterly was "The Shark at the Window," accepted by the *Sewanee Review* in 1947 or 1948 and published in 1951. This event was greeted with awe and excitement by his fellow students and also by me. I wrote my first piece for the *Sewanee* in 1949, about Allen Tate's criticism, and then more reviews and two essays about Auden. Three years later, in 1952, through a concatenation of events I won't go into here, I became editor of the magazine. By this time Dickey had finished his B.A. and M.A. at Vanderbilt and gone to teach at Rice, but had been called back into service after a few months because of the Korean War. He then returned to teach at Rice from 1952 to 1954. As soon as I took over the editorship, I invited him to send me his poetry; and when the Rockefeller Foundation made a grant to *Sewanee* and three other quarterlies enabling us to award fellowships to promising young writers, I invited Dickey to apply. With the enthusiastic concurrence of my advisory editors, Allen Tate, Andrew Lytle, and Francis Fergusson, I gave him a fellowship that enabled him to leave Rice, which he did not find very sympathetic, and go to Europe for the first time, where he spent a year.

I must enter the pedantic mode here to correct a few errors that have crept into some published accounts of these matters. While I invited and encouraged Dickey to write regular essay-reviews and to send me his own poetry, it is not true that he was ever poetry editor nor even any sort of official or exclusive poetry reviewer for the *Sewanee Review.* The magazine did not operate in that way; there was no such delegation of authority. But it is certainly true that I took great pride and satisfaction in publishing him as frequently as possible. There was no connection whatever between Dickey's first appearance in *Sewanee* and my own, and no connection between his teaching at Rice and my leaving Sewanee for Rice in 1964.

Some reviewers of Dickey's recent *Collected Poems* have assumed that all the poems in the first section, "Summons," are previously unpublished. This is not true: at least twelve of the twenty-five poems were published in various magazines from 1954 to 1964. It seems to me unfortunate, I may note in passing, that these poems have been added while thirteen of the nineteen poems in *Puella* have been dropped; the early poems are certainly not without interest, but the ones lost from *Puella* are far superior as poems.

I will now gladly abandon the biographical and pedantic modes and make a few observations about Dickey's poetry as a whole. Dickey is peculiarly difficult to "place" or classify or evaluate, for two main reasons. In the first place, he has always been independent, a loner, not identified with any group or program or tendency. In the second place, he has argued that change is a good thing, and has put this belief in practice, for during his career his poetry has undergone a number of pronounced, though not fundamental, changes.

Dickey has never been indifferent to or unaware of his readers, as some visionary poets—Blake or Rimbaud, for instance—have appeared to be. On the contrary, he has always been determined to get his readers involved: it has been a cardinal principle of his poetics that the poem is not merely an object to be contemplated but an action or process to be participated in by the reader—a spell or incantation or ritual or prayer. In his public readings he has been extremely successful in getting very large audiences to participate fully and enthusiastically, and his poems appealed to unusually large numbers of readers even before *Deliverance* and its movie and the coffee-table books made him a household word. One critic calls him a "pitchman" for poetry, but this word suggests the cheap and fraudulent rhetoric of the snake-oil salesman or carnival barker; Dickey's word "barnstorming" is much better, suggesting adventurous and sometimes dangerous activity done mainly for the fun of it. It is the fact that Dickey is so successful at it that most annoys his detractors; he makes large popular audiences enthusiastic about poetry that is on the surface often peculiar and even outrageous. When he does this, he is in no sense prostituting the poetry, but bringing it into the real world and seeking the largest possible audience for it, as every poet surely wants to do.

Twenty-odd years ago, in my *Dionysus and the City* (a book so long out of print it may be unknown to many of you), I discussed Dickey's poetry in terms of the Dionysus-Apollo polarity first defined in Nietzsche's "Birth of Tragedy." His poetry is, I argued, a good example of the fruitful tension between the Dionysian principle of striving toward transcendence of the human, going beyond art and rationality and civilization to achieve ecstasy and vision, and the Apollonian principle of order, form, proportion, in art; restraint, moderation, and civic responsibility in conduct. Though his themes are primarily Dionysian—metamorphosis and transfiguration, the sense of the nonhuman (animals and birds) and the more-than-human, the wisdom of excess and drunkenness, that which breaks down barriers, goes beyond reason and common sense and individualism, that which can be touched but not known— his Apollonian qualities help to explain why Dickey, unlike so many Dionysian poets, has been able not only to survive but to develop. He has never attempted to dispense with form or to oversimplify its difficulties, as many more extreme Dionysians have. In spite of the openly autobiographical aspect of much of his work, he is not a confessional poet: the experiences he describes are universal, not peculiar to the individual. While the Dionysian aspect is most obvious in Dickey, I said, the Apollonian is there too, and one would not work without the other. I still think this is a good way to approach Dickey, though it is hard to sum it up briefly without reducing it to truisms like the necessity of both energy and restraint, vision and form. I used it again a dozen years later in my essay on Dickey as Southern Visionary and Celestial Navigator, in which I dealt mostly with *The Zodiac* as the end of the Dionysian line and with *Puella* as a shift back toward the Apollonian.

In subsequent years the Apollonian aspect of Dickey's poetry has become more and more prominent. (His criticism, which is outside my territory in this discussion, has always provided massive testimony of the power and refinement of his Apollonian side.) Several of the poems in *The Strength of Fields* celebrate public occasions and public figures. A poet takes a real risk when he undertakes such commissions; but Dickey has never been reluctant to take chances. There are some disasters in these public poems, but a remarkable number of successes; it is a difficult genre. Eulogies, fulsome praise, hype of all sorts—these are hard to avoid and absolutely deadly. Dickey's strategy is usually to say nothing directly about the occasion or the person being celebrated, but instead to deal with their mythical aspects in the largest terms. The title poem, "The Strength of Fields," was read at the inauguration of President Carter in 1977 and "Apollo" about the astronauts who orbited and then landed on the moon. "Exchanges," the last and, in the opinion of many, the finest poem in the volume, was written for an occasion only slightly less public, as the Harvard Phi Beta Kappa poem for 1970. The poem is a tribute to Joseph Trumbull Stickney, a proper Bostonian who nevertheless appreciated California, and who (by the way) wrote the moving lines on his approaching early death from brain cancer: "Sir, say no more. / Within me 'tis as if / The green and climbing eyesight of a cat / Crawled near my mind's poor birds." It also adapts some of Stickney's best lines to current themes, such as pollution (destroying the "gentle ecstasy of earth") and the moon landing: "Apollo springing naked to the light." It sums up many of the themes of the volume and makes very clear Dickey's sense of responsibility to society, his concern for America's violation and pollution of the natural environment.

But the title poem, "The Strength of Fields," is, for me, even more haunting and suggestive. For a public poem, it is curiously indirect and oblique, totally lacking in the expected eulogy of its subject, and instead meditating on two of Dickey's central themes: the nature and function of the hero and the nature of fields, in many senses but primarily of the American land itself. The hero, as Dickey sees him, has a social function: he separates himself from the world to penetrate to a source of power, and returns to enhance life. And, we realize, this is exactly what an American president does, or hopes to do, at least if he is an idealist like Jimmy Carter. He will draw strength from our patriotism and kindness, and this will renew our nation like the renewing green of the earth. Dickey's last line, "My life belongs to the world. I will do what I can," is taken, as he has pointed out, from a story by Alun Lewis, a British poet killed in World War II. It is perfectly appropriate for Carter, and the historical irony that Carter's administration was a political disaster and was succeeded by Reagan's adds to the pathos of the line.

The title poem of Dickey's next volume, "The Eagle's Mile," celebrates the death of Justice Douglas and "For a Time and Place" the inauguration of Governor Riley of South Carolina. The volume seems to me more tightly organized than any preceding one, so much so that most of the poems operate as sequences in which the context is an important part of the meaning. The central theme might be said to be *place:* the effect of different regions, climates, geological formations on human beings, or in the broadest terms, the relation between man and his environment, external nature. The line "Let the place talk," from "Circuit," might serve as description of them all. The places range from the arid semi-desert Southwest—presumably New Mexico—in the beginning to the graveyards and tombstones of the end, when there are curious and suggestive dialogues with the earth and with the moon and its white world of death. (In Dickey's new novel, *To the White Sea,* there are spiritual exchanges or *participations mystiques* with rocks, trees, running water, ice, snow, and wind, and with rabbits, lynxes, martens, and especially hawks, that often resemble these poems in interesting ways.)

In form, the poems are often approximations of the ode, never formal or pretentious but impersonal lyrics, descriptive and meditative, and often with a strong consciousness of social responsibility. The style of many of them is somewhere between Gerard Manley Hopkins and Walt Whitman—or sometimes, as in "Eagles," resembles both at once. (We remember Hopkins's famous remark that he knew in his heart Walt Whitman's mind to be more like his own than any other man's living. "As he is a very great scoundrel this is not a pleasant confession.") The emphasis on sound, and repeated figures of sound, is strongly reminiscent of Hopkins.

The thematic center of the careful arrangement of poems in *The Eagle's Mile* seems to me to be the title poem and the following one, "Daughter." The title poem celebrates Justice Douglas as hero, one-eyed like Wotan or Orion, gaining power from his injury, champion of nature as environmentalist, preservationist, and strenuous outdoorsman, an eagle compared to most men's antlike stature, and like the eagle capable of taking a view larger than the personal. The mythologized figure of Douglas presides over the whole volume. In the title poem, Dickey imagines Douglas as being resurrected in the annual resurrection of his beloved nature and rising "straight up / In the eagle's mile"; "Let Adam, far from the closed smoke of mills / And blue as the foot / Of every flame, true-up with blind-side outflash / The once-more instantly / Wild world: over Brasstown Bald / Splinter uncontrollably whole."

The next poem, "Daughter," describes the poet awaiting the birth of his daughter, as he sits in the hospital waiting room with a man with an "injured eyeball." When he sees his newborn daughter, he says "wordlessly / Roll, real God. Roll through us." He exults in the movement of nature, "lava, the flowing stone," the slow but "irrevocable millennial inch" of the glacier's movement, and concludes: "All forests are moving, all waves, / All lava and ice. I lean. I touch / One finger. Real God, roll. / Roll." Then follows, to take the curse off this exalted revelation, the comic and self-deprecatory "The Olympian."

The poem on the inauguration of Governor Riley says nothing whatever about the governor, but deals entirely with the climate, topography, fauna, and flora of South Carolina, and the effect of these on the state's inhabitants. It is accurate, penetrating, and often funny, far more entertaining than any eulogy: "What visions to us from all this lived / Humidity? What insights from the blue haze alone? From kudzu? / From snake-vine? From the native dog-sized deer . . . ?" "It is true, we like our air warm / And wild, and the bark of our trees / Overlapping backward and upward / Stoutly . . ." Some of the prose essays in *Night*

Hurdling provide a gloss on or amplification of the poem, especially "The Starry Place Between the Antlers." Dickey remarks there that what convinced him to come to South Carolina was the university president's comment that he would like it if he liked flowers and birds.

Much of this poetry has a strong element of comedy, often self-deprecatory; and comedy is, of course, a social art, requiring the writer to see himself and his society from outside. Many of these poems, too, involve conscious imitation, and often affectionate parody, of other poets. A good example is "The Olympian," a "False Youth" poem in which Dickey (no persona here) plots to win a race against his son's teacher, a former Olympics champion.

> He came lankily, finely drawn
> Onto my turf, where all the time I had been laying
> For him, building my energy-starches,
> My hilarious, pizza-fed fury. My career of fat
> Lay in the speed-trap, in the buckets and tools of the game-plan,
> The snarls of purified rope. Then dawned the strict gods of Sparta,
> The free gods of Athens! O lungs of Pheidippides collapsing in a square
> Of the delivered city! O hot, just hurdlable gates
> Of deck-chairs! Lounges! A measured universe
> Of exhilarating laws! Here I had come there I'd gone
> Laying it down confusing, staggering. . . .

The form, though not technically Pindaric, recalls Pindar's odes in praise of athletes, with stylistic traces too of Hopkins's odes of praise; the middle-aged father goes down to defeat, but he's been a contender. It seems to me a wonderfully funny and touching poem.

It is rare for a visionary poet to have the capacity for comedy, and especially self-ridicule: you won't find it in Poe or Rimbaud or Crane, but you will sometimes in Dickey's special hero Roethke. Dickey's humor is more frequently present than most people seem to realize, but its most characteristic form is the preposterous lie or grotesquely implausible vision that outrages the reader, but then turns out to be, in a deeper sense, true and meaningful. Among his earlier poems, "Approaching Prayer" is a good example of Dickey's conscious absurdity meant seriously. His awareness that he looks foolish by commonsense everyday standards emphasizes his deliberate flouting of them. His aim is to remythologize and remystify poetry; his conception of it is the polar opposite of Eliot's early description of poetry as a "superior form of amusement." But he is capable of the light touch. "Power and Light" is perhaps his wittiest poem, based entirely on word-play but nevertheless serious, defining his concept of the energized man. Beginning with the special electrical meaning given to E. M. Forster's "only connect" as the epigraph, it seems to me extremely funny and extremely meaningful.

Dickey's poems about the war in *The Strength of Fields* are partly comic: "Haunting the Maneuvers," for instance, and "Camden Town" as a poem of "flight-sleep." The "False Youth" poems seem to me successful in this genre, especially "Autumn: Clothes of the Age," which is also both an *ars poetica* and a credo. At the end, the poet faces down the ridicule of the barbershop rednecks as he puts on his foxtail hat and displays the back of his jacket:

> And there it is
> hand-stitched by the needles of the mother
> Of my grandson eagle riding on his claws with a banner
> Outstretched as the wings of my shoulders,
> Coming after me with his flag
> Disintegrating, his one eye raveling
> Out, filthy strings flying
> From the white feathers, one wing nearly gone:
> Blind eagle but flying
> Where I walk, where I stop with my fox
> Head at the glass to let the row of chairs spell it out
> And get a lifetime look at my bird's
> One word, raggedly blazing with extinction and soaring loose
> In red threads burning up white until I am shot in the back
> Through my wings or ripped apart
> For rags:
> *Poetry.*

The tone is perfect, and the bedraggled one-eyed eagle and the dangling foxtails the perfect comic symbols for Dickey's poetry.

Translation, "imitation" in the eighteenth-century or Robert Lowell sense, and collaborations of various kinds—these are all, of course, highly Apollonian activities (though come to think of it, nothing could be more explicitly Apollonian than Dickey's treatment of the Apollo space flights)—and these, too, have been occupying much of Dickey's time. Dickey's titles for these pieces are scrupulously exact in describing just what he is doing: "Free-Flight Improvisations from the unEnglish" instead of "translations," and "Head-deep in Strange Sounds" to indicate a primary concern with sound. Similarly, "Double-tongue" calls attention to the dialogue element implicit in "Collaborations and Rewrites"; not, heaven forbid, dueling banjos again, but a topic of considerable interest to close readers.

Especially in *Deliverance* and *Puella,* but also in the poetry we have been discussing, Dickey might be called the poet who redeems suburbia by reaffirming its connection with the wild rather than its sterile isolation. The Call of the Wild may sometimes yield temporarily to the summons of Apollo; but it will never die out in his work. As Hopkins said, "O let them be left, wildness and wet; / Long live the weeds and the wilderness yet."

Dickey has always been an easy target; he won't keep his head down and he is highly vulnerable. But the *Collected Poems* make the shape and magnitude of his accomplishment plain. He is unlike anyone else; he has had a powerful influence on the public at large as well as on the small audience most poets have nowadays. He has made poetry seem vital and important, not merely a superior form of amusement or a purely aesthetic activity, but related to the central activities and experiences of life.

At Vanderbilt the relationship between Dickey and me was limited and rather impersonal: we didn't talk about ourselves, but rather about poetry and such related matters as philosophy and the other arts. Of course I did recognize Dickey's remarkable talent and his great promise, and I was very glad I was in a position to help his career along a little when I became an editor. But I hadn't realized how much our talks at Vanderbilt meant to him until he began making public statements about it in the latter sixties, going into some detail in *Self-Interviews,*[1]

1. *Self-Interviews* (Garden City, N.Y.: Doubleday, 1970).

and dedicating *Falling*[2] to me. We have met occasionally over the years, usually when one of us is performing, as I did at the celebration of his sixtieth birthday here ten years ago, then he did at my retirement in Houston three years later; and both of us spoke at my induction into the South Carolina Academy of Authors in Charleston earlier this year. He never seems to tire of telling how much he learned from me, and I certainly never tire of hearing it. But now the time has come at last for me to acknowledge that I have learned from him over the years far more than he can ever have learned from me. I will always be proud to have had some part in his development, for though I cannot say, as Matthew Arnold said in response to Keats's wistful statement, "I think I shall be among the English Poets after my death," "He is—he is with Shakespeare," I can say the American equivalent: he will be among the American poets, with Whitman and Frost, Eliot and Stevens, Robert Penn Warren, Hart Crane, and Theodore Roethke.

2. *Falling, May Day Sermon, and Other Poems* (Middletown, Conn.: Wesleyan University Press, 1981).

CHAPTER 6

~

Auden Twenty Years

After: A Question

of Poetic Justice

TWENTY YEARS AFTER Auden's death, it is obviously time for reinterpretation and reassessment of his poetry from a later perspective. Though Auden seems still to be popular with the intelligent general reader, is frequently quoted, and is certainly of continuing interest to biographers and scholars, few students seem to find him very exciting, and few critics are stirred by his poetry or his ideas. (Some even find fault with his homosexuality as insufficiently assertive.) David Perkins, for example, says, "To the extent that Auden's poetry survives, it will be the poetry of the thirties, with much of the later verse noticed primarily 'in a scholar's footnote.'"[1] Ashbery, Merrill, and Zukovsky he finds much more interesting.

How very fortunate we are, then, that the task of revaluation should be undertaken not by an ambitious critic eager to use Auden to demonstrate his own ingenuity, political correctness, or learning, but by one of the best poets living, who writes not to advance any theory, but as a tribute and labor of love. Anthony Hecht, in *The Hidden Law: The*

Published in the *Sewanee Review,* summer 1994.

1. David Perkins, *A History of Modern Poetry: Modernism and After* (Cambridge and London: The Belknap Press of Harvard University Press, 1987), 169.

Poetry of W. H. Auden (Harvard University Press, 1993), accepts the full responsibility of the critic, however, old-fashioned as well as "new": he considers the poetry with the utmost seriousness and intellectual rigor, and supplies the contexts and backgrounds—biographical, literary, social, intellectual—necessary for full understanding. His central concern is to provide the fullest, richest, and most perceptive readings that he can of the poems that he loves and admires most. Using terms not often encountered in today's criticism, he expresses throughout his own delight in and gratitude for Auden's poetry.

This is a book of an extremely rare kind, and perhaps even unique: a full-length reading and discussion by a major poet of the work of an immediate predecessor, a dominant figure whom he knew in person and whose work was an important influence on his own. One may say of Hecht what Dr. Johnson said of Dryden, that his "is the criticism of a poet; not a dull collection of theorems, nor a rude detection of faults, which perhaps the censor was not able to have committed; but a gay and vigorous dissertation, where delight is mingled with instruction, and where the author proves his right of judgment by his power of performance."

Regardless of one's opinion of Auden, to read this book is a liberal education: it is to meet, in its author, a richly cultivated mind, sensitive and wide-ranging, and a generous spirit that is nevertheless firmly moral and realistic. But the special virtue of the book is its interpretation of a very important poet's work by a younger poet of very different background and temperament but comparable stature. A cat may look at a king, and many critics fit this feline image; but when one king looks at another the results are likely to be more interesting and significant.

Like Auden, Hecht is a poet in the grand tradition: not so modern that he regards the past as a joke, but committed to assimilating the whole past history of English poetry and the whole European tradition of civilization and confronting responsibly the perennial major issues of morality, politics, and religion, as well as art. But he is, again like Auden, no solemn pontificator, but frequently witty and amusing, and a virtuoso of meter and the other formal aspects of poetry. He does not fall into the trap of praising most those aspects of Auden's work that are most like his own: he maintains a certain generous but real detachment. He takes Auden's ideas seriously and makes every effort to understand and explain them sympathetically; but he does not hesitate to express disagreements. He seems to have in mind a reader who is intelligent, knowledgeable, and a committed lover of poetry; but who has no special knowledge of Auden and will welcome both helpful information and close and subtle reading. Hecht's chief aim is to enrich and clarify the reading of the specific poems, though he does not by any means shirk discussion of the questions raised by them.

The focus, then, is on the poetry, though Hecht makes full use of all available biographical sources insofar as they help with the reading. (He makes good use of the books by Harold Norse, Dorothy Farnan, Charles Miller, Alan Ansen, Nicholas Jenkins, and others, as well as Humphrey Carpenter's standard biography.) He is particularly good on Auden's homosexuality, neither exaggerating its importance nor minimizing it, but handling it sensitively and compassionately.

Some of Auden's poems are to be fully understood only by the addressee; in them, as in some of Shakespeare's sonnets, there is "extreme intimacy of address to a solitary reader" (109). "In Praise of Limestone," for example, which overtly defends an antipuritanical ideal and repudiates Manichaean dualism, also bears on a private relationship. This relationship (with Chester Kallman) "was not, for the most part, a happy one, and one of the tasks Auden seems to have set himself was to write about it with enough 'distancing' and objective impersonality to avoid self-pity, or even any clear indication that he was writing about himself." He had already done so in "The Temptation of St. Joseph" (in *For the Time Being*) as well as elsewhere, and later writes short lyrics embodying this attitude, such as "Deftly, admiral, cast your fly," which Hecht analyzes as tragedy. Hecht quotes Carpenter: "Chester's behaviour was not simply a betrayal of a love-affair but a breaking of what Auden regarded as marriage vows" (313).

Auden was under no illusions about the joys of homosexuality. "I've come to the conclusion that it's wrong to be queer, but that's a long story. . . . In the first place, all homosexual acts are acts of envy." Elsewhere, Auden says "few, if any, homosexuals can honestly boast that their sex-life has been happy" (180). Hecht is, I think, right in exposing Auden's defense of homosexual prostitution as a sentimental daydream, pathetic but false. "Finally, most personally and most touchingly of all, there appears to be a growing distance in the new poetry between a dream of reciprocated love and of sexual happiness on the one hand, and a presentation of desire or of sexual intercourse that is increasingly coarse and brutal (though some would simply call it frank) and almost despairing. . . . And as his faith in the possibility of a reciprocated love began to fail ('If equal affection cannot be, / Let the more loving one be me'), he found himself writing about the subject in terms that were cold, self-protectively remote, fearful of self-pity, and generally distrustful" (296). Hecht cites such examples as "Minnelied," "The Platonic Blow," the Hugerl poems, and "The Willow-Wren and the Stare," contrasting these with W. B. Yeats's "Solomon and the Witch," where sex brings revelation.

Many British critics seem never to have forgiven Auden for his apostasy in coming to America and avoiding the war, and some lingering Leavisites still speak of Auden's "inverted development." A good many Americans have been inclined to such views by Randall Jarrell's essays and reviews purporting to expose the incoherence and confusion of Auden's changing ideas as well as the collapse of his style. Hecht begins with what seems to me a very astute move: he confronts immediately these brilliant but hostile pieces of Jarrell's, which still do great damage to Auden's reputation and may have been partly responsible for Auden's odd decision to arrange his *Collected Poems* of 1945 according to alphabetical order of first lines. Hecht does not make a blanket defense, but points out the extraliterary animus in Jarrell's disapproval of Auden's changing political and religious stance and also the oedipal element in Jarrell's violent rejection of Auden as literary father-figure; and from this Hecht moves into his own admirably balanced account of Auden's early poetry and subsequent development.

The Hidden Law is, for me, compulsively readable and continuously fascinating. It is a sad example of the lack of interest in reviewing poetry or criticism of poetry nowadays that this book, the fruit of a major poet's lifetime reading of and meditation about an older poet of central importance to our times for four decades, should have received so little recognition. The few reviews I have seen have conveyed little sense of just how extraordinary it is. (The *New York Times Book Review,* for example, printed only a contemptuous dismissal in about 250 words, by a person unknown to me who seemed ignorant of both Auden and Hecht.)

Hecht happened to be resident at the same time (1950) as Auden on the island of Ischia, and became acquainted with him then, though he had known and admired his work for the preceding decade. His most extended piece about Auden before the present book was an essay on "In Praise of Limestone," first published in 1979 and reprinted in his volume called *Obbligati*.[2] (The landscape and setting of "In Praise of Limestone" is, of course, primarily Ischian.) This essay was a highly successful experiment in a critical mode Hecht self-deprecatingly compared to collage: collecting all relevant material that casts light on the poem (including passages from Auden's other poems and prose and from a wide variety of other sources), with minimal comment by the critic. This present book retains the unhurried, leisurely, personal tone of the earlier piece and its method of quoting at length from all relevant material, but is more economical, more sharply focused and more tightly organized.

Hecht's purpose is not to exorcise any "anxiety of influence," but to express his own delight in and gratitude for Auden's poetry, and in doing so to enhance and enrich the reading of Auden by others. Hecht's reading is personal, but it is also critically responsible in that he scrupulously considers all relevant contexts and is anything but dogmatic: he states his own opinion candidly, but supplies the material for the reader to make up his own mind.

Hecht's discussion of Auden's elegy on Yeats is a good example of his approach. Instead of taking a high aesthetic line in defending Auden's famous (or notorious) assertion that "poetry makes nothing happen," Hecht first cites inoffensive parallel statements by Northrop Frye ("Poetry is a disinterested use of words") and Keats ("We hate poetry that has a palpable design upon us"). But as the "definitive gloss" on Auden's line, and on the whole question of propaganda poetry, he quotes Howard Nemerov's "On Being Asked for a Peace Poem":

2. *Obbligati: Essays in Criticism* (New York: Atheneum, 1986).

Here is Joe Blow the poet
Sitting before the console of the giant instrument
That mediates his spirit to the world.
He flexes his fingers nervously,
And resolutely readies himself to begin
His poem about the War in Vietnam.
This poem, he figures, is
A sacred obligation; all by himself,
Applying the immense leverage of art,
He is about to stop a senseless war.
So Homer stopped that dreadful thing at Troy
By giving the troops the Iliad to read instead;
So Wordsworth stopped the Revolution when
He felt that Robespierre had gone too far . . . (146).

Hecht does not deny that Auden has faults (he is particularly severe on his sloppy and misleading punctuation, and he disapproves of most of Auden's revisions), but he takes the view that such flaws do not deprive a poem of value, and he invokes both personal and larger historical perspectives. Objecting to the deletions and revisions in "September 1, 1939," he adds:

Nevertheless, like many poetry readers of my generation, I continue to be enormously grateful for this poem. No one else took it upon him- or herself to address directly and unequivocally the massive crisis that was inevitably to become the Second World War. There were, in the course of time, some other war poets, some of them very good; but either they wrote about personal experience with warfare, or they wrote with a deliberate metaphoric distancing, as Eliot did in the quartets. Auden addressed the crisis at its inception, regarded it with historical perspective that in no way diluted the force and horror of its importance; made the crisis psychological, personal, and universal, and did so in passages that are nothing less than memorable. I feel sure that many others share with me the sense of the timely importance of this poem, and who [sic] cherish it as I do for a literary monument. I was just coming to military age when the war began. Like many another, I can remember all the anxiety those headlines generated. And Auden gave them wonderful voice. To say this is not to say that the faults in the poem are negligible . . . (152).

To remind us of the historical perspective, Hecht even spells out the chronology of the "low dishonest decade."

One outstanding virtue of Hecht's book, not surprising but gratifying, is its awareness of contemporary poetry and its illuminating discussions of Auden's relation to such poets as Eliot, Yeats, Frost, Nemerov, Roethke, Wilbur, and William Plomer. Hecht is concerned not with such trivial questions as that of "influence," but with matters of belief and morality as well as technique, and his penetrating comparisons often cast much light on both poets being considered. For example, in his extensive and brilliant discussion of *For the Time Being,* he finds traces of Eliot's "very puzzling doctrine" that "it is better, in a paradoxical way, to do evil than to do nothing: at least we exist" (271). (Eliot, we remember, made this remark in defending Baudelaire, and suggested a parallel in Dante's detestation of the neutral angels.) But Hecht takes the doctrine seriously into the real world and exposes its falsity: there is no neutral ground.

> Failure to do good is not "doing nothing"; it is doing harm. And when Eliot proceeds to embrace the paradox that "it is better to do evil . . . than to do nothing," it seems to me he is entering upon grounds where I cannot follow him, and suspect him of being in grave danger. I should not myself care to defend the position that the mass murders of Stalin and Hitler were in any way morally superior to some form of human behavior . . . that could be described as "morally neutral." To do nothing may be wicked, but to classify active crime as "morally superior" to it seems to me a sophistical exercise in perversity. And there was that in Eliot that was always attracted to the perverse (273).

There is a curious parallel between Auden and Eliot in that traces of another paradox are to be found in both: that poetry is "fundamentally frivolity." It is ironic that the brief review of Hecht in the *New York Times Book Review* should pick up and misinterpret that phrase. While the reviewer quotes Auden correctly as saying "poetry is fundamentally frivolity," she ignores his next sentence, which explains it: "The only serious thing is loving God and your neighbor" (175); "Everything that isn't required of you is fundamentally frivolous." This notion is similar to Eliot's definition of poetry as "superior amusement"; but Eliot, too, offers immediate clarification: "I call it amusement . . . not because that is a true definition, but because if you call it anything else you are likely to call it something still more false." Hecht suggests, I think rightly, that both statements are reactions against Matthew Arnold's notion of art as substitute for religion: "There are times when it almost seems that Auden still regards Arnold as the most dangerous heretic around." He speaks of "Auden's half-seriously entertained doctrine about the essential frivolity of art, only religion being worthy of serious and solemn meditation . . . a doctrine that Auden himself could not have completely believed," and jokes about "the pleasure of debating whether it is to Byron or to Eliot that Auden owes his views" (177). In his later years, of course, Auden became almost obsessively concerned that his poetry be, above all things, truthful.

Hecht's evaluations are implicit in his choice of works for extended discussion. He neither defends those he finds less successful nor wastes time spelling out their defects. (He does not, for example, have much to say about *The Dance of Death* or *The Orators* as whole works, nor about anything after *The Shield of Achilles* [1955]. *The Sea and the Mirror* he dismisses as static and undramatic, and *The Age of Anxiety* as "a kind of daring, and not wholly successful, experiment.") While Auden's admirers might wish to rise to the defense of any or all of these slighted pieces, they will surely be gratified that Hecht's selectivity allows him time for unhurried discussion of what he finds central in Auden.

The discussions are admirably thorough, but wholly unpedantic, often personal and amusing. Hecht takes Auden seriously, in the best sense: he explains Auden's ideas and beliefs sympathetically, but then does not hesitate to give his own opinion on the questions involved as well as his own reactions to the poems. After considering the 1930 *Poems*, Hecht has a splendid chapter on *On This Island* and *The Dog Beneath the Skin*. This is followed by the longest and arguably best chapter of all, on *Another Time*. Subsequent chapters deal with the *Letter to Lord Byron, New Year Letter,* and *For the Time Being*. (Hecht's is by far the best commentary ever written on this crucial and enormously complex "spoken oratorio." I agree with his implied judgment that it is Auden's greatest single work.) Chapters follow on *Nones* and *The Shield of Achilles*. The final one, "The Hidden Law," more a speculation or epilogue than a formal conclusion, returns to the epilogue of *The Orators* to suggest a unifying theme.

My chief problem in writing this review has been to avoid language that seems extravagant or inflated and therefore always provokes a skeptical reaction in the reader, who naturally suspects extraliterary motives or senses the clouds of puffery and hype always threatening in the literary atmosphere. But I cannot conceal my own delight and satisfaction in seeing Auden get his due at last in a critical book worthy to stand beside the poetry, both illuminating it and restoring Auden to his proper place among the great poets of our century. Hecht's book is in itself a constant pleasure to read, free of all pedantry, and filled with helpful information and reflections sometimes amusing and often profound; it is also an invaluable companion and guide to Auden's work. Hecht's last chapter, "The Hidden Law," gives the book its title; its thesis may be very crudely summarized as the belief that ultimately truth will out and poetic as well as other justice will be done. The reception of Hecht's book so far confirms that the law remains well hidden; but I have no doubt that it will continue to operate and the truly exceptional virtues of *The Hidden Law* will eventually come to be fully recognized.

CHAPTER 7

∾

Reynolds Price:

Passion and

Mystery in Fiction

WHEN REYNOLDS PRICE was stricken with cancer in 1984, he felt an extraordinary renewal of inspiration. Since then he has produced three plays, a volume of poems, a remarkable collection of essays called *A Common Room,* and his most popular novel, *Kate Vaiden. Good Hearts* (1988), his delightful and thought-provoking seventh novel, is the continuing fruit of this renewal. (By 1992 he had published a ninth novel, *Blue Calhoun.*)

Though *Good Hearts* is a sequel to Price's first novel, *A Long and Happy Life,* published twenty-six years earlier, it is almost twice as long and very different in style and tone. *A Long and Happy Life* was a pastoral, describing the courtship of Rosacoke Mustian, a simple but very intelligent country girl, and Wesley Beavers, her womanizing, motorcycle-riding, ex-navy lover. She does what she thinks she needs to do to keep him. When she finds herself pregnant, Wesley is willing (but not eager) to marry her; the resolution of the novel comes when she, playing the part of Mary in a Christmas pageant, accepts her role.

Good Hearts takes up the same couple again, after some thirty years of marriage. In contrast to the pastoral isolation of the first novel, the

Based on reviews in the *Washington Post,* April 10, 1988, and the *Raleigh News and Observer,* June 27, 1993.

characters in this one live very much in the contemporary world, in the small city of Raleigh. Rosa works as secretary to a university English department and Wesley as a mechanic (only on expensive foreign cars). Wesley, now fifty, leaves Rosacoke and goes to Nashville, where he finds a mistress. Rosacoke is raped (in consequence, it is suggested). The story is pulled along irresistibly by suspense (will Wesley return? will Rosacoke take him back? will the rapist make another attempt?). When Wesley does return after a few months, it remains uncertain whether or not he will stay and whether or not Rosacoke will take him back; finally she does. As to the rapist, he does at last return, but as a guest in the house, and blesses the marriage.

Good Hearts is more readable than *A Long and Happy Life:* the style is simpler, closer to contemporary speech; there are no more long, dreamy sentences to evoke a pastoral world, no idyllic distancing, but more suspense and more dialogue. Price can write dialogue that seems natural but characterizes economically without awkwardness or dialectal spelling; Rosa, especially, is highly distinctive both in speech and in her writing in her diary. Whereas *Life* was told by an omniscient narrator, *Hearts* uses varied methods of narration: after an omniscient beginning chapter, Rosacoke tells her story through her diary, which alternates with the omniscient presentation of Wesley's story. When Wesley comes home the omniscient narration continues, but Rosa's diary has established her as the protagonist and as the articulate character, as opposed to Wesley, who doesn't like talking but has the touch for both machines and women.

The title, *Good Hearts,* is plausible enough for Rosa and Wesley; on the basis of both this novel and the earlier one, we readily agree with the omniscient narrator of the first chapter that they have "hearts as good as any you've met unless you meet more saints than most." Rosa has her flaws, but is a very sympathetic character, overcoming the comic archetype of woman as pursuer—which she embodies throughout both novels, in which from first to last she pursues Wesley. Wesley is gentle, incapable of causing deliberate harm (here he is unlike D. H. Lawrence's nonverbal men who have the touch); he causes Rosa pain, but his leaving her is, we are led to believe, a necessary result of his character. He feels, understandably enough, at fifty, that he has always been essentially passive, has never defined himself. But Wesley remains a mythical character, somewhat enigmatic, not to be captured by language.

To make the reader believe in the goodheartedness of the rapist, Waverly Wilbanks, however, is the most difficult task Price has set for himself. Waverly believes that he is helping women by raping them; his motive is entirely altruistic and religious, and he requests thanks from his victims. In the final chapter, Wave explores Rosa and Wesley's bedroom just before they return to it. He finds a mysterious resemblance between himself and a picture of Rosa's father, and hears the voice of God telling him that what he has done has been right.

The sense of the supernatural is strong throughout; though never defined, it is felt as unquestionably real. There are mysterious connections and coincidences, as between Wesley's leaving and the rape, and Rosacoke's brother Rato's dream that tells him when Rosa is being hurt. Everybody in the novel prays regularly, though their beliefs vary widely. Wesley says of Rosacoke's profession of belief in the Apostle's Creed and the Lord's Prayer, "Don't be a damned missionary all your grown life," and of his own beliefs, "Oh, I guess there's a God. But it sure as hell looks like He's so far gone, He can't see us and barely hears even our loudest begging." Emma, Rosa's mother, is happy because she concludes finally that there is no heaven or hell after death, "No eternal glare on her tired eyes, no big reunion of all her old kin, grinning and singing and ready to eat," but rest, pure rest, which is what she yearns for. On the other hand, Wave, the benevolent rapist, has as his favorite text, "I consider that the sufferings of this present time are not worth comparing with the glory that is about to be revealed to us."

Price's characters seem real people that one can identify with and take seriously; they are responsible and make significant choices. They want to be good, do what is best for each other. If Waverly is not wholly convincing (at least to this reader) and Wesley remains somewhat remote, Rosacoke is fully realized and vividly present. She is not perfect, but she is warm and loving as well as dutiful and good, and she is intelligent and funny as well as shrewd. In the end she accepts Wesley's need to change, as he accepts her need for permanence.

While *Good Hearts* is self-sufficient, much is added to it if the reader goes back to *A Long and Happy Life,* for the later novel casts light on the earlier, as well as vice versa. At the end, the reader has the sense that all has been resolved and explained as well as may be in a universe that, if full of mysteries still, makes fundamental sense.

In the title essay in *A Common Room,* Price makes a plea for a kind of Authors Androgynous, for the novel as a common room for the understanding of both sexes. The heroine he has created, Rosacoke, is a triumphant example of such understanding.

Thirty years after his first volume of stories, *The Names and Faces of Heroes* (1963), Reynolds Price has included in *The Collected Stories* everything in it and his second volume, *Permanent Errors* (1970), together with an equal number of stories written since his interest in the form revived a few years ago. Let me say immediately that this collection is a rich, varied, and fascinating one, indispensable to anyone interested in Price's career, in Southern literature, or in serious fiction of any place or time.

To describe the book so conventionally may be misleading, however, for Price, though certainly serious—an eminent professor, novelist, and man of letters, a deeply religious writer preoccupied with the ultimate questions of life and death—is also often comic and outrageous, with a highly individual attitude toward sex and the supernatural, among other things. He means to shock and disturb the reader, not to amuse him. Of his own basic impulse to fiction, Price says, "From the start my stories were driven by heat—passion and mystery, often passion for the mystery I've found in particular rooms and spaces and the people they threaten or shelter."

I happened to have been reading Peter Taylor's *The Oracle at Stoneleigh Court* just before Price's book, and the two collections make an interesting contrast. Taylor's stories are complex, ironic, subtle; a supernatural element is invoked in many of them, but it is no more than a hint or a possibility—that, in the title story, the old lady may have been able really to foretell the future, or that the Owl Mountain witch may somehow have caused the deaths of those who betrayed her. But in Price's stories we often meet the supernatural face to face and undisguised. A favorite theme is an encounter with an angel, as when an adolescent boy peering through a hole in the bathroom door is vouchsafed a revelation of the glory of sex—both sexes—by an angel with feathers. Where Taylor is interested primarily in the "normal" concerns of people like you and me, Price is interested in strange and extreme mental states—suicidal depressions, hallucinations, visions, deaths and rebirths, healings, spiritual exchanges. Taylor's attitude is carefully distanced, even when the subject is quasi-autobiographical, and his narrators are notoriously unreliable; Price, on the other hand, is often explicitly autobiographical, and his narrators obvious masks of himself. His aim is moral or religious rather than aesthetic: in the words he likes to quote from Rilke, he wants to make the reader change his life.

Price is not much concerned with verisimilitude; as he has remarked, his fiction is often more like romance (in the old meaning) than like the realistic novel. His problem, therefore, is to make the reader believe in it, at least for the moment; for if the reader is not willing to suspend his disbelief, he will not be moved or changed by the experience. Let us take a few examples. "The Enormous Door," already mentioned, describes a twelve-year-old boy's epiphany of the glory of sex, revealed through a hole in the bathroom door. Most of the details are convincing: the bathroom is in a hotel, and is occupied by a teacher in the local high school; his sexual partner is a female teacher; the transfiguration witnessed by the boy is believable, though the feathers remain a mystery. But the apparition convinces the boy, precisely because it is unlike conventional representations of angels, and at sixty he still finds the experience a genuine revelation: he is "the last man alive, so far as I've heard, to whom a god unquestionably came and showed the sacred joy that waits in any human body, if it has the wild courage to find its adjoining door and kneel to its chink." And thus his somewhat grotesque and embarrassing search for sexual knowledge is made meaningful and blessed.

Even more grotesque is "The Company of the Dead," in which the narrator, now ninety-two, recalls "setting up" for pay with the body of a dead girl when he was fifteen. The boy's attitude—macabre, slightly erotic, fearful, joky—is well established, and then the girl's guilty lover appears, demanding that her corpse tell him whether or not he should live. "Then something obeyed him—our Maker or a demon or Mariana her shining self, wherever she roamed," and she says "No." He cuts his throat, and the narrator comments, "Love—this force commended by

God and Christ his Son as the height of virtue—will freeze one life and char the next; no way to predict who lives or dies. No lover thrives or ends with flesh and mind intact, uncharred and smiling." And he tells us that he has always been careful to avoid "the pointed stakes of love"—and has thereby impoverished his life.

"Watching Her Die" again presents a narrator looking back to his boyhood, recalling his first guilt at his own gratuitous act of cruelty. He confesses it to his aged and somewhat goofy aunt, who says she must die for him, and proceeds to do so while he watches. But his father revives (or resurrects?) her. The narrator learns that "You can somehow choose to pay the debts of a needy boy or other grown soul if you have that much to give and are willing," and comments that "since Aunt Lockie paid all for me . . . I've never doubted my place in the world or my endless duty to find at last the needful heart for whom one day I lay my own life down and depart." In contrast to the other narrator, who learned the wrong lesson, this one has learned (in wholly nontheological terms) the meaning of a central Christian doctrine.

Though Price arranges the stories in this volume in a nonchronological order based on "alternation of voices, echoes, lengths and concerns," the stories I have mentioned are all among the later ones. Though in some ways more daring, they do not seem to me quite as powerful as "Fool's Education" and "Walking Lessons," which I should call his finest achievements in the form. As in Eudora Welty (who has been one of Price's chief mentors and models), love and separateness are the basic polarity in these stories: failure of love is the deepest fault, but love has its dangers and sharp edges, and separateness is necessary, especially for artists. Price's stories are deeply felt and deeply meant; but they do sometimes strain the bounds of credibility: if the reader can't really believe them, then they can't be truly meaningful to him or involve his emotions. At his best, however, Price justifies the risk and brings it off triumphantly.

CHAPTER 8

~

Schubert, Keats,

and the True

Voice of Feeling

THOUGH MUSIC AND sweet poetry must needs agree because they are sister and brother (as the poet Richard Barnfield affirmed), attempts to define relations and analogies between poets and composers have not been notably rewarding. The relations between the late quartets of Beethoven and those of Eliot are certainly important; but it is not easy to go beyond what Eliot himself has said. There are obviously suggestive analogies between, say, Pope and Mozart, or Berlioz and Byron, or Debussy and Mallarmé, or Shakespeare and subsequent composers from Purcell to Prokofieff; but to go beyond large generalizations is difficult and of doubtful value. The analogy between Keats and Schubert, however, seems to me to constitute a special case. (There was certainly no specific relation between the two; though they were almost exact contemporaries—Keats 1795–1821, Schubert 1797–1828—it is extremely unlikely that either of them ever heard of the other.) Schubert united poetry and music in creating a new art form, the Lied, and in other musical forms as well established an intimate emotional relation to his hearer like that of the poet to his reader. Maurice Brown describes his "poetic approach to the composing of music. He wished to feel intensely, and to express to the utmost of his powers, the present moment in his music: not for its significance as a link with what has gone and what is to come, but for its momentary effect as sound, as pleasure for the listener."[1] Keats's verbal art resembles music in its direct and immediate emotional effect; "O for a Life of Sensations rather than of Thoughts!,"[2] he writes in a famous letter, and "I look upon fine Phrases like a Lover."[3] His sensitivity to music appears in such references as "The music, yearning like a God in pain" in *The Eve of St. Agnes* and in his private system of alternating vowel sounds. There is reason to hope, then, that juxtaposing these two artists may prove illuminating.

Schubert and Keats are now among the most accessible of great artists: the works of both the poet and the composer are immediately appealing, with abundant beauties that anyone can appreciate (and therefore may sometimes dismiss as overly familiar). Unfortunately, these attractions, so obvious to us, were not sufficient to bring much money or fame to either in his lifetime. Schubert was handicapped by not being highly gifted as either performer or conductor, as all the other great composers were, and had no powerful patrons to help him. Keats lacked Byron's flamboyance and aristocratic connections and Shelley's financial backing, political passion, and gift for outrageousness. He tried to write plays, and his *Otho the Great* (a Shakespearean tragedy written in collaboration with Charles Brown) was almost produced, but the plans fell through. The three volumes of his poetry published in his lifetime (1817, 1818, 1820) received little notice, and much of that unfavorable. His fame began with Shelley's well-meant but misleading *Adonais,* representing him as slain by hostile reviewers, which provoked Byron's comment in *Don Juan:*

> John Keats, who was killed off by one critique
> Just as he really promised something great
> If not intelligible, without Greek
> Contrived to talk about the gods of late
> Much as they might have been supposed to speak.

1. Maurice J. E. Brown, *Schubert: A Critical Biography* (London: Macmillan; New York: St. Martin's Press, 1958), 196–97.

2. Maurice Buxton Forman, ed., *The Letters of John Keats,* 3d ed. (London, New York, Toronto: Oxford University Press, 1947), 69.

3. Ibid., 368.

Poor fellow! His was an untoward fate;
'Tis strange the mind, that fiery particle,
Should let itself be snuffed out by an article.

Keats's reputation was greatly enhanced when his moving, profound, and immensely attractive letters were published by Monckton Milnes in 1848, together with his *Literary Remains* and a biography; and were followed by Milnes's publication in 1856 of *The Fall of Hyperion*. It was confirmed by the admiration of Tennyson, Browning, and Matthew Arnold. But his full stature was recognized only in the twentieth century. As Aileen Ward well says, "Keats's work has survived better than that of any of his contemporaries the long devaluation of romantic poetry that began about the time of Auden's appearance on the scene."[4]

As for Schubert, though he was admired by a wide circle of friends, primarily as a writer of Lieder and piano pieces, his major works were neither performed nor published in his lifetime. Schumann discovered the Great C Major Symphony in 1839 and Mendelssohn conducted it; but the "Unfinished" Symphony was not discovered until 1865. Much of the chamber and piano music and hundreds of Lieder were not published until long after Schubert's death (and the same is sadly true of his operas, his chief bid for fame and fortune). The great C Major Quintet, for example, was not performed until 1850 and was published in 1853; the three great piano sonatas of his last year were not published until 1838. Liszt, Brahms, Sir George Grove, and Sir Arthur Sullivan all took part in the discovery of Schubert that continued for the rest of the century.

Schubert and Keats are alike in that they are both unquestionably and centrally Romantics, but without the characteristics that have given Romanticism a bad name. Their Romanticism may be described in Milton's classical terms: their art is "simple, sensuous, and passionate." Their aim is to express emotion as powerfully, but also as precisely, as possible, while remaining simple and direct. They can express sentiment without the least trace of sentimentality; they can express emotions without self-consciousness or embarrassment. They seek "the true voice of feeling."

4. Aileen Ward, *John Keats: The Making of a Poet* (New York: Viking Press, 1963), 414.

(The phrase was used by Keats in a letter explaining that he had decided to give up his Miltonic *Hyperion* because it had too much of "the false beauty proceeding from art" and not enough of "the true voice of feeling."[5]) But the true voice, as it appeared in the revised version, *The Fall of Hyperion: A Dream,* was strongly influenced by Keats's study of Dante; the feeling was not limited by the simplicity. In both Keats and Schubert, feeling is balanced by an active and powerful intelligence.

Both men had very attractive personalities; they were not self-absorbed, humorless, and egotistical like many Romantics. Both came from relatively humble backgrounds; both were single-mindedly devoted to art, though with great capacity for friendship and love. Neither married; both died young and, aware of the imminent approach of death, strove desperately to fulfill their artistic ambitions before they died. Keats writes, "I am certain of nothing but of the holiness of the Heart's affections and the truth of Imagination."[6] Matthew Arnold said he had more felicity of language, "natural magic," than any poet except Shakespeare. Schubert has immense sensuous appeal through his moving and delectable melodies, which seem inexhaustible in variety and quantity. These melodies are as irresistible as is Keats's sensuous and luxuriant beauty of sound and image.

Schubert, though so spectacularly gifted as melodist, was not lacking in sense of form; each Lied fulfills all the formal demands of music while remaining true to the meaning of the poem. His architectonic sense is fully evident in his longer compositions—piano sonatas, string and various other trios, quartets, quintets, octets, symphonies, masses, operas. Keats, on the other hand, did not live long enough to write the kind of long poems that he intended to, though his greatest odes and sonnets certainly lack nothing of formal perfection.

Both Keats and Schubert were centrally concerned with the human and dramatic. Keats was determined to write Shakespearean plays, but he was unsuccessful in *Otho* mainly because he was versifying a foolish plot by his collaborator, Brown, and was never able to try again except in the brief fragment *King Stephen.* Schubert in his operas (*Alfonso und*

5. Forman, ed., *Letters,* 385.
6. Ibid., 67.

Estrella and *Fierrabras* were his most ambitious) was handicapped by atrocious librettos, but he was enormously successful in his songs, and the dramatic element was essential to their success. In the first place, Schubert's elevation of the pianist's role to equality with the singer's made for drama, and often there are two persons in the song, or two aspects of the same person, in conflict. Early examples are the piano accompaniment, suggesting the spinning-wheel's varying speeds and rhythms in counterpoint to Gretchen's emotions, in *Gretchen am Spinnrade,* and the alternating voices of the Erlking and the child in *Erlkönig,* or Death and the Maiden in *Der Tod und das Mädchen.* The piano's suggestion of the storm outside, paralleling the singer's emotion, is highly effective in *Erlkönig* and *Die Junge Nonne.* The highly developed dramatic quality is, of course, essential to the song-cycles *Die schöne Müllerin* and *Winterreise.*

Schubert was genuinely modest: his lifelong and closest friend, Josef von Spaun, described him as "a loyal and affectionate friend, . . . in the highest degree modest and obliging, in spite of the fact that he was not unconscious of the worth of his achievements; and he was graced with the lovely characteristic that the success of others never made him jealous; he rejoiced over every success and if his worst enemy had composed something beautiful, he would have been delighted about it. He did not know what envy was."[7] He shunned virtuosity, wrote no concertos, and did not like to conduct or perform in public. (Aside from the piano, his instrument was the viola.) What he preferred is what came to be called the Schubertiad: informal and noncompetitive performances before a private roomful of close friends and invited guests. (In our time, extended public performances of Schubert's music are now often called Schubertiads, and flourish annually from Feldkirch in Austria to the Ninety-second Street Y in New York.)

Schubert's credo, *An die Musik* (1817), shows his modesty and lack of egotism:

> Du holde Kunst, in wieviel grauen Stunden,
> Wo mich des Lebens wilder Kreis umstrickt,

7. Otto Erich Deutsch, ed., *Schubert: Memoirs by His Friends* (New York: Macmillan, 1958), 361–62.

Hast du mein Herz zu warmer Lieb entzunden,
Hast mich in eine bessre Welt entrückt!

Oft hat ein Seufzer, deiner Harf' entflossen,
Ein süsser, heiliger Akkord von dir
Den Himmel bessrer Zeiten mir erschlossen,
Du holde Kunst, ich danke dir dafür!

(O blessed art, how often in dark hours, when the savage ring of life tightens round me, have you kindled warm love in my heart, have transported me to a better world! Often a sigh has escaped from your harp, a sweet, sacred harmony of yours has opened up the heavens to better times for me. O blessed art, I thank you for that!)

Maurice Brown says the melody of this Lied is "as truly Schubertian as anything he wrote—intimate, ardent, and with that indefinable touch of pathos which goes to the heart."[8] This observation applies equally well to Keats, who sees tragedy in beauty—"beauty that must die"— and opposes it to philosophy, which would "unweave a rainbow," and sometimes to reality, as the knight in *La Belle Dame* awakens "on the cold hillside."

According to Dietrich Fischer-Dieskau, the greatest modern performer of Schubert Lieder, *An die Musik* often concluded Schubert's own Schubertiads.[9] The setting of Goethe's *Der Musensohn* (1822) takes a more lighthearted view of the poet's (and musician's) art. (Schubert set thirty Goethe poems in 1815 alone, including *Erlkönig*. It is not really surprising that Goethe did not respond when these were sent to him; no doubt he thought the poems were good enough already, and self-sufficient.) Schubert had a remarkable understanding of and feeling for all kinds of poetry, responding to greatness (Goethe, Heine, Schiller) but often making merely competent poetry into great Lieder. The obvious examples are the two great song cycles, *Die schöne Müllerin* and *Winterreise,* based on sequence-poems by Wilhelm Müller that no one would call great. Müller's poetry is, however, more complex than

8. Brown, *Schubert,* 77.
9. Dietrich Fischer-Dieskau, *Schubert's Songs: A Biographical Study* (New York: Limelight Editions, 1984), 83.

it appears in Schubert's Lieder. For example, in *Die schöne Müllerin* Schubert omits Müller's Prologue, Epilogue, and some other poems in which the author appears in his own person as puppet-master and distances himself ironically from the drama. These add interest to the poetry, but are impossible to set to music. Another example is the poem just discussed, *An die Musik*. Its author, Franz von Schober, was Schubert's friend but a very undistinguished poet, who nevertheless this one time wrote well and truly. Like Keats, Schubert knows how to distinguish true feeling from false, and is never self-deceived.

Keats, as his letters show, was similarly modest as a person, aware of and honest about his own defects and those of his egotistical contemporaries. His attitude toward his art was similarly reverential and grateful, as in the great sonnet in which the metaphor for reading is traveling in realms of gold, and discovering Chapman's Homer is like discovering a new planet or the Pacific Ocean. *Bards of Passion and of Mirth* imagines poets as leaving their souls on earth to inhabit a new heaven, and in a lower key, this charming early sonnet describes the shared joy of reading with friends:

> Keen, fitful gusts are whisp'ring here and there
> Among the bushes half leafless, and dry;
> The stars look very cold about the sky,
> And I have many miles on foot to fare.
> Yet feel I little of the cool bleak air,
> Or of the dead leaves rustling drearily,
> Or of those silver lamps that burn on high,
> Or of the distance from home's pleasant lair:
> For I am brim-full of the friendliness
> That in a little cottage I have found;
> Of fair-haired Milton's eloquent distress,
> And all his love for gentle Lycid drowned;
> Of lovely Laura in her light green dress,
> And faithful Petrarch gloriously crowned.

Both came from the lower middle class (Keats's father was a coachman who became a livery-stable owner; Schubert's was a music teacher in a school), and suffered some ridicule and condescension on this account, especially since their diminutive stature (both were just over five feet) and, in Schubert's case, insignificant appearance, could also be ridiculed. "Little Johnny Keats" of the Cockney School of Poetry (also called "Pestleman Jack," practitioner of poetry and pharmacy) and Schubert, the little mushroom ("Schwammerl" was his more or less affectionate nickname), shy and awkward in society, lacking poise and presence—such were the wounding terms used by their detractors. Mozart, Haydn, and Beethoven had aristocrats as patrons and sometimes friends—archdukes, counts, even prince-archbishops—while Schubert's friends were penniless artists or poets, or at most well-to-do singers, and the evenings that were called Schubertiads were dominated by the piano in a private home. The entertainment would consist often of Schubert at the piano, singing or playing his own compositions—accompanying singers of his Lieder, playing impromptus or sonatas solo or duets with others or waltzes for the company to dance to. Keats's friends were, except for Leigh Hunt and the painters Haydon and Severn, not distinguished or public figures; Shelley made generous but uncomprehending gestures toward him, but Wordsworth did not, though Keats reverenced and admired him, and Byron, as we have seen, ridiculed *Adonais,* while tepidly praising *Hyperion.*

Because both received so little recognition and so much condescension in their lifetimes, Keats and Schubert evoke a special kind of protective tenderness and enthusiasm in their admirers. Schubert is still not properly recognized by the general public, and to become acquainted with the full range of his art gives a special sense of discovery; with Keats, going beyond the best-known poems and reading the letters makes us want to respond, when Keats writes, "I think I shall be among the English Poets after my death," as Matthew Arnold did: "He is; he is with Shakespeare."

Both differ from their contemporaries in being deeply traditional rather than rebellious, looking back to the major exemplars of their art. It is the art itself, not the expression of their personalities, that is important to them. This is most obvious in the case of Keats, who is inspired by Dante, Spenser, Drayton, Shakespeare most of all,

Milton, and Dryden. Aileen Ward says: "In an age in which, by its best critics at least, originality was exalted far above tradition, Keats's special originality was his sense of dedication to the whole tradition of English poetry and his attempt to recover it for the use of poetry in his time."[10]

Of his Romantic contemporaries, he admires Wordsworth most. But Wordsworth was no such towering, overwhelming presence to Keats as Beethoven was to Schubert. Keats reveres Wordsworth, and compares him to Milton, who "did not think into the human heart, as Wordsworth has done";[11] "we find what he says true as far as we have experienced and we can judge no further but by larger experience—for axioms in philosophy are not axioms until they are proved upon our pulses."[12] But he is aware of Wordsworth's limitations and personal defects: "I am sorry that Wordsworth has left a bad impression where-ever he visited in town by his egotism, Vanity, and bigotry. Yet he is a great poet if not a philosopher."[13] He contrasts his own poetical character (a chameleon, without self or character, identifying with other things and people) to the "wordsworthian or egotistical sublime."[14]

Schubert managed to avoid being dominated by Beethoven, though he fully recognized his greatness and learned much from him. At the beginning of his career, when he was fourteen and had already composed a great deal, he confided to his friend and schoolmate Spaun, "Secretly, in my heart of hearts, I still hope to be able to make something out of myself, but who can do anything after Beethoven?"[15] He dedicated a set of variations for the piano to him in 1822, signing himself "your admirer and worshipper Franz Schubert," but never met him unless (according to an unreliable source) he visited him on his deathbed in 1827; at any rate, it is certain that he was one of thirty-six torchbearers at Beethoven's funeral. As Maurice Brown observes, "It is Schubert's chief glory that he could be contemporary

10. Ward, *Keats*, 415.
11. Forman, ed., *Letters*, 144.
12. Ibid., 142.
13. Ibid., 107.
14. Ibid., 227.
15. Deutsch, ed., *Schubert: Memoirs*, 128.

with a dominating figure like Beethoven, without slavishly imitating him."[16]

Alfred Brendel, as pianist one of the great modern interpreters of Schubert, has written well on this topic:

> The idea that Schubert tried to model his sonatas on Beethoven's and failed has nevertheless confused many a listener. . . . Arnold Schoenberg knew better . . . he emphasizes Schubert's "inconceivably great original-ity in every single detail next to a crushing figure like Beethoven". . . . Schoenberg's admiration for Schubert's "self-respect" is boundless: "Close to such crushing genius, Schubert does not feel the need to deny its greatness in order somehow to endure. What self-confidence, what truly aristocratic awareness of one's own rank which respects the equal in the other!"

Brendel continues:

> Schubert relates to Beethoven, he reacts to him, but he follows him hardly at all. . . . The character Beethoven presents is one of defiance based on firmness of musical proportion. Schubert presents an energy that is nervous and unsettled . . . ; his pathos is steeped in fear.[17]

Following in the path first explored by Arthur Schnabel as both performer and critic, Brendel reveals and interprets the greatness of Schubert's piano music, especially the last three sonatas. Other great pianists of other traditions than the Germanic have in recent years made glorious and beautiful interpretations of Schubert's piano works: Maurizio Pollini, Radu Lupu, and András Schiff, for example.

Like Keats, Schubert had a good but limited education and therefore was determined to continue to educate himself in the traditions of his art throughout his life. His friend Josef von Spaun said that he "possessed the most thorough musical knowledge and had studied the works of the great masters, both old and new, in the greatest detail.

16. Brown, *Schubert,* 196

17. Alfred Brendel, *Music Sounded Out* (New York: Farrar, Straus & Giroux, 1991), 137–38.

Bach and Handel he worked through thoroughly and held in very high esteem; all Gluck's operas he could play almost from memory and there was probably not a note by Mozart, Beethoven and Haydn that he did not know."[18] It is touching that he was taking lessons in counterpoint and attending a course on fugue at the time of his death. Keats wanted to learn Greek and worked at it regularly until September 1819, when he gave it up but continued to study Italian. As late as November 1820, Shelley, with typical lack of realism, intended to teach Keats Greek and Spanish.

Their most striking biographical similarity, as I have already suggested, is that both died young and wrote their greatest works under the shadow of approaching death. Working in a foreshortened and speeded-up time scale, both rapidly became mature and, of necessity, tragic artists; but, for both, fame was largely posthumous, not fully achieved until long after death.

The greatest difference between them is suggested by their respective epitaphs. Keats wrote his own, with a despairing realization that he would not have time to realize his full potentialities: "Here lies one whose name was writ in water." (His friends softened this in the actual inscription on the gravestone: "This Grave contains all that was Mortal of a YOUNG ENGLISH POET Who on his Death Bed, in the Bitterness of his Heart at the Malicious Power of his Enemies, Desired these Words to be engraven on his Tomb Stone 'Here lies One Whose Name was writ in Water.'"[19]) In other moods he can believe that he will "be among the English Poets after my death" or transcend the question in a great sonnet: "When I have fears that I may cease to be / Before my pen has gleaned my teeming brain, / . . . —then on the shore / Of the wide world I stand alone, and think / Till love and fame to nothingness do sink." (This sonnet, written in 1818, was not published until 1848.) But the sad fact is that he had a mature writing life of only four years at most: his first great poem ("Chapman's Homer") was written in 1816, but most of the great poems were written in the single year 1819, after which he was too weak to write. Splendid though his achievement was,

18. Deutsch, ed., *Schubert: Memoirs,* 362.
19. Ward, *Keats,* 406.

he simply did not have time to get all the wine into the bowl (to use a metaphor from Pound). Even Matthew Arnold felt obliged to judge that his achievement was "partial and incomplete."

Schubert's case, fortunately, was different. Born in 1797, he was more precocious, as musicians often are. By the time he was seventeen, he had written two symphonies, five string quartets, four operas, a mass, and some of his most famous songs. *Gretchen am Spinnrade,* written in 1814, was his first real masterpiece; Maurice Brown says this, his first setting of Goethe, marked

> the appearance in music of the first great German song in the sense understood today. . . . Never before in music had a poem so deeply and sincerely felt been matched with music as deep and sincere. *Gretchen* may claim to be the first song in which the music presents and explains the words in a fashion that the poet-dramatist could not, even though that poet be Goethe. The way in which the monotonous figure in the pianoforte accompaniment, which is a musical symbol of the spinning-wheel, stops at the climax of the song, when the girl's transport robs her of the power of physical movement, is unforgettable; but so, too, is the broken, sobbing resumption of that figure on the piano, for Schubert gives us here not only the spasmodic starting of the spinning-wheel, but the painful return of everyday sensation after the tranced numbness of the girl's body.[20]

Keats's first masterpiece, the sonnet on Chapman's Homer, was written just before his twenty-first birthday; his friends saw that it "announced the new poet taking possession."[21] Schubert, as we have noted, was only seventeen when he composed *Gretchen.* He began his career much earlier than Keats, lived to be thirty-one, and so had a mature career of at least fourteen years as compared to Keats's four. Schubert had the strength to compose many of his greatest works in his last years. Keats, on the other hand, was too sick to accomplish much after October of his one great year, 1819. He called the tubercular attack of February 1820 his "death-warrant," and spoke thereafter of his "posthumous existence" until his death in February 1821.

20. Brown, *Schubert,* 28.
21. Ward, *Keats,* 77.

Grillparzer's epitaph engraved on Schubert's tombstone, "The art of music here entombed a rich possession but even far fairer hopes," expresses an undeniable truth—who knows what Schubert might have gone on to do had he been able to continue?—but also gives the false impression that he had been cut off before he had realized his potential, fulfilled his hopes, or produced any masterpieces other than songs. (Most of his greatest works, as I have already said, were unperformed and unpublished until long after his death.) The Viennese public promptly forgot what little they had known of him, and it was not until the end of the century that all his works were rediscovered and available, and well into the present century before they began to receive anything like their due appreciation.

In Keats a central theme is the incompatibility of beauty and truth, as in *Lamia,* where cold philosophy, which would "unweave a rainbow," "clip an angel's wings," reveals Lamia's true nature, coupled with betrayal by woman, as in *La Belle Dame.* Beauty is associated with death, as in *Ode to Melancholy,* Art is beautiful and permanent but dead, as in *Ode on a Grecian Urn.* So his work is implicitly tragic. But Keats did not have time to work these themes out fully, as Schubert did.

Schubert was fortunate in having enough time to complete his aesthetic and spiritual voyage, or so it would seem: it is hard to see where he could have gone beyond the supreme works of his last seven years, beginning with the "Unfinished" Symphony and the "Wanderer Fantasy" of 1822 and continuing with the *schöne Müllerin* song-cycle of 1823; the Great C Major Symphony, once dated 1828 but now shown to be 1825–1826; the last three string quartets (traditionally numbered 13, 14, 15—in A Minor, D Minor ["Death and the Maiden"], and G Major), 1824–1826; the two piano trios, the *Impromptus* and *Moments musicaux* for piano; and the incomparable *Winterreise* song-cycle in 1827. In the final year alone, 1828, there were the C Major Quintet (which Thomas Mann called "the music one would like to hear on one's deathbed"), the three last piano sonatas, *Drei Klavierstücke,* and the *Schwanengesang* collection of songs. The *Winterreise,* and especially the last song, *Der Leiermann,* is the supreme example of Schubert's acceptance of tragedy, in the bleak, frozen music of the hurdy-gurdy man. But this acceptance is equally apparent in the Great C Major Symphony, where it is balanced by a vigorous, resolute, almost martial theme, and in the C Major Quintet, where it is transformed into an ethereal, meltingly beautiful slow movement, and in the last movement takes on a manic, whirling gaiety.

Keats, in addition to writing the great odes and sonnets in 1819, continued to make progress in his longer poems: the couplets of *Lamia,* influenced by his study of Dryden, are a great advance over those of *Endymion,* and *The Fall of Hyperion* gets out of the Miltonic shadow of *Hyperion* and does succeed in expressing the "true voice of feeling" more adequately than the earlier version. (As the strong influence of Dante, especially the *Purgatorio,* indicates, more is involved than feeling alone: the mood of the *Fall of Hyperion* is one of tragic acceptance.) But he lacks the strength to write after the fall of 1819. Keats foresaw as early as 1817 that he "must die / Like a sick eagle looking at the sky," and expressed his frustration directly, with bitterness and agony, in the late letters.

Had he lived longer, would he have continued to develop? Some critics feel that Keats would not have been able to go further even if his health had held out, that he was caught in the insoluble dilemma of the Romantics and despaired because he was honest and clear-sighted enough to see the dilemma for what it was. E. E. Bostetter, for example, says: "Finally, under no circumstances could poetry achieve the importance or do the things he demanded of it. There is the possibility that, finding himself unable to write poetic drama with conviction or effectiveness, he would simply impatiently have given up poetry except for incidental composition and turned to writing for the periodicals, or abandoned writing altogether like Rimbaud." "Beyond doubt by the end of 1819, independent of illness and love, he was spent as a poet. . . . Keats recognized the necessity of healing himself before he could be the physician poet . . . In his passionate devotion to poetry lay both the sources of his power and its potential frustration. When he spoke of 'those abstractions which are my only life' he was speaking literally, and yet he could not refrain from a restless, intellectual questioning of them which was certain to undermine his belief in their validity."22 (John Jones, in his perceptive *John Keats's Dream of Truth*,23 comes to a similar conclusion.)

Aside from terminating them, what effect did disease have on the careers of both men? Keats contracted a venereal disease (the latest opinion is that it was probably gonorrhea rather than syphilis) in 1817, then tuberculosis in 1818; he predicted then, accurately, that he would live only three more years. After the great year of 1819, he was unable to write any more poetry. (As we have seen, there may have been other reasons besides health.) Schubert contracted syphilis in 1822, and some critics think that this shock may be partly responsible for the daring innovations of the "Unfinished" Symphony late in the same year and for the deepening and often darkening tone of much of his work from this time forth. At any rate, it did not prevent his subsequent development and the composition of an enormous quantity of music, climaxing in his final year of 1828, when he produced his greatest works.

Thomas Mann has explored perhaps more thoroughly than anyone else (except Freud) the relation between disease and art, especially in *The Magic Mountain, Death in Venice,* and *Doctor Faustus.* Mann's Faustus sold his soul to the Devil by contracting syphilis and with it a spell of immense artistic creativity. For the German Romantics, "disease is a mark of spiritual distinction," in contrast to "stupid, healthy life," as Erich Heller puts it.24 In a letter of 1818, Keats says: "Until we are sick, we understand not;—in fine, as Byron says, 'Knowledge is Sorrow'; and I go on to say that 'Sorrow is Wisdom'—and further for aught we can know for certainty 'Wisdom is folly'!' "25 Art itself is like a disease, separating the artist from ordinary life and depriving him of a sense of identity; this theme Keats explores occasionally in his letters. The line between physical and spiritual malaise is tenuous. Nietzsche said that an artist thrives on conditions that are "akin to, and organically connected

22. Edward Everett Bostetter, *The Romantic Ventriloquists* (Seattle: University of Washington Press, 1963), 176–77, 179.

23. John Jones, *John Keats's Dream of Truth* (New York: Barnes & Noble, 1969).

24. Erich Heller, *The Ironic German: A Study of Thomas Mann* (Boston & Toronto: Little, Brown, 1958), 202–4.

25. Forman, ed., *Letters,* 142.

with, the pathological, so that it seems impossible to be an artist without being sick."[26] Nietzsche's own syphilis and the tuberculosis ("consumption") of Chopin, Chekhov, and D. H. Lawrence are examples of the possible link between disease and artistic stimulus. Shelley, urging Keats to come to Italy, refers to the link between disease and artistic stimulus as an accepted fact: "This consumption is a disease particularly fond of people who write such good verses as you have done."[27] But the effect of disease for both Keats and Schubert seems to have been primarily psychological rather than physiological: confrontation with mortality and the awareness of imminent death stimulated both into desperate activity and also forced the acceptance of a tragic view of life.

Keats in *Hyperion* represents Apollo's assumption of power as tragic:

> Knowledge enormous makes a God of me. . . .
> Soon wild commotions shook him, and made flush
> All the immortal fairness of his limbs;
> Most like the struggle at the gate of death
> Or liker still to one who should take leave
> Of pale immortal death, and . . .
> Die into life: so young Apollo anguished.

In the *Fall of Hyperion,* the tragic theme is even more explicit: Moneta tells the poet (who has assumed Apollo's role in his own person) that "None can usurp this height . . . / But those to whom the miseries of the world / Are misery, and will not let them rest." They "are no dreamers weak, / They seek no wonder but the human face; / No music but a happy-noted voice"; and the poet replies, "sure a poet is a sage; / A humanist, physician to all men. . . . / The poet and the dreamer are distinct." He disdains "all mock lyrists, large self-worshipers, / And careless Hectorers in proud bad verse."

Keats, then, may have been unable to continue *The Fall of Hyperion: A Dream* or to write effectively after it not only because of his health but also because he was unable to maintain belief in the central Romantic credo: that the imagination, not discursive reason, is the instrument

26. Heller, *Mann,* 203.
27. Forman, ed., *Letters,* 505.

of truth and that dreams are as valid as waking reality. He affirms this credo frequently, as in the 1817 letter stating as his only certainties the "holiness of the Heart's affections and the truth of Imagination,"[28] "What the imagination seizes as Beauty must be truth," or, in the famous affirmation of the Grecian Urn, "Beauty is truth, truth beauty." But Keats is too honest and too realistic to believe that poetry is effective either as individual therapy or as an agent of social good; the dreamer and the physician-poet that he would like to be remain quite distinct. *Lamia* shows that beauty is not truth; *The Fall of Hyperion* is *A Dream*. Keats associates beauty instead with death; Melancholy "dwells with Beauty— Beauty that must die; / And Joy, whose hand is ever at his lips / Bidding adieu, and aching Pleasure nigh, / Turning to poison while the bee- mouth sips."

Aileen Ward suggests that Moneta, in *The Fall of Hyperion,* sums up this most compelling image in all Keats's poetry: her "wan face" is that of the

> Goddess of Memory, who has gazed for ages with infinite compassion on the sufferings of the world; it is also the Goddess of Melancholy whom he had met . . . in the Temple of Delight. Yet it is also the pale lady of the disastrous wedding feast, La Belle Dame, Auranthe with eyes "semi- shaded in white lids," Lamia staring at her lover without recognition . . . it is the open-lidded star and the moon . . . that presided over his earlier poetry, but whose gaze is now recognized at last and forever as sightless. In the end it is the face of death itself, in the most beautiful and terrifying aspect in which Keats had met it—the face of his dead mother, shrouded for her coffin. . . . It is the very foundation of Keats's poetic structure, the metamorphoses recurrent throughout his poetry of the "Beauty that must die" and the dead miraculously brought to life again; it suggests the driving force behind the metamorphoses of his own identity. The boy whose heroic assertiveness was formed in protest against his mother's faithlessness, the adolescent who became a doctor in half-conscious expiation of his failure to save her from death, the young man who first turned to poetry to escape the memory of her suffering but became a true poet in facing and accepting the burdens of his own identity— now at last in his fullest self he confronts the experience that so greatly

28. Ibid., 67.

shaped him and regards it with love and pity, not with terror. In his discovery of beauty in the face of death Keats emerged as the poet who is "Physician to all men." Here he finally proved himself capable of the poetry he had dreamed of writing; yet these were almost the last lines he ever wrote.[29]

Lamia and *The Fall of Hyperion* show a part, at least, of what Keats might have done if he had had more time; but the latter, fine as it is, is only a beginning, a fragment. Keats was intensely aware of being cut off; he wrote to Fanny Brawne in 1820: " 'If I should die,' said I to myself, 'I have left no immortal work behind me—nothing to make my friends proud of my memory—but I have loved the principle of beauty in all things, and if I had had time I would have made myself remembered.' "[30]

Schubert was not cut off before he had fulfilled himself, though his greatest works, and the great bulk of his work, remained unperformed and unpublished until long after his death. Keats, on the other hand, left few important works to be discovered posthumously except *The Fall of Hyperion*, a few sonnets, and the letters—though they, when published by Monckton Milnes in 1848, gave his reputation a tremendous boost. (His letters to Fanny Brawne, however, in the opinion of Matthew Arnold—betraying a touch of Victorian class-consciousnesss—should not have been published, being "underbred and ignoble.")

Beethoven is often portrayed as a Titan, voicing defiance against the gods and the existing order in heaven as on earth. Schubert is also a gigantic figure, independent and often innovative; but not this kind of defiant rebel. Though he did do a brilliant setting of Goethe's dramatic *scena, Prometheus,* he is more like Keats's fallen Titans in *Hyperion* and *The Fall of Hyperion:* contemplative, often melancholy, but philosophical in recognizing the necessity of change. Keats never mentions Prometheus, defiant creator of and fire-bringer to mankind, the archetypal Titan hero of most of the Romantics, unbound in Shelley's play, celebrated in Beethoven's ballet-music *The Creatures of Prometheus.*

29. Ward, *Keats,* 340–41.
30. Forman, ed., *Letters,* 468.

In contrast, Keats's Titan heroes are the defeated Saturn and the fallen Hyperion. "We begin to live when we have conceived life as tragedy," Yeats says in his *Autobiography*,[31] and Nietzsche celebrates "tragic joy"; Schubert is triumphant, not defeated, in his tragic acceptance. Like Keats, Schubert fully appreciates ordinary human life, celebrating its everyday beauty and joy as well as its heights and depths. Of his last two songs, *Die Taubenpost* has, in Richard Capell's words, a "sunny ingenuousness and almost jaunty lilt,"[32] and *Der Hirt auf dem Felsen* is equally cheerful. This strain, with renewed vigor and resolution, is as prominent as the solemn and tragic in the other great compositions of his final year. Keats's *Ode to Autumn* and his last sonnet, "Bright star! Would I were steadfast as thou art," show a similar calm acceptance of death as part of life.

31. William Butler Yeats, *Autobiography* (New York: Macmillan, 1953), 116.
32. Richard Capell, *Schubert's Songs* (New York: Macmillan; London: Duckworth, 1957), 257.

CHAPTER 9

∾

A

Happy

Induction

THE LAST ORGANIZATION I was inducted into, more than fifty years ago, was the Army of the United States; the present induction will, I trust, have less dramatic consequences. It is certainly much pleasanter. According to the Bible, a prophet is not without honor, save in his own country. I suppose I am a kind of prophet in a small way (the modern term is "cultural critic"); yet here I am being honored in my own country. I am therefore tonight an exceptionally fortunate and happy man.

Tonight I propose not to venture into real autobiography but to risk a few personal speculations—but not so personal as to be embarrassing—about some of the people and other influences that were responsible for making me what I was and am. I have until now avoided autobiography partly because, to begin writing, I would have had to choose one among the multiplicity of perspectives from which any life may be seen, at each stage or as a whole. Every event may be seen as either random or part of a significant pattern, and every choice as either inner-directed or a function of time and place. There can be no universal or eternal

On being inducted into the South Carolina Academy of Authors, Charleston, March 1993.

114

view; the autobiographer must write at a specific time and in a specific place, each dictating its own needs, pressures, and emphases, and thus affecting the interpretation. I must acknowledge the influence of the present time and place in producing a rather euphoric mood, tempered by a mild sense of grievance that the publication of my last book seems to have been a very well-kept secret.

W. H. Auden said that a poet or novelist who wrote his own auto-biography was shortsightedly spending his capital rather than prudently living off his dividends. But I have arrived at an age when I no longer need worry about going into capital. With advancing age one becomes aware of oneself as a relic, a survivor, an exhibit, if not a monument, in the imaginary museum of time and thus willy-nilly a part of history. My grandmother was born in 1848, and brought me up on tales of the Civil War and its aftermath; my father was born in 1874, experienced the depression of the 1880s, the Populist movement of the 1890s, and the boom of the 1920s; he died just before the stock market crash of 1929. I was born in 1916, dimly remember World War I and the Roaring Twenties, and vividly remember the Depression, World War II, and everything thereafter up to the present nineties, which one hesitates, for several reasons, to call gay. As one becomes a part of history, one feels a responsibility to testify, to help put the right caption on the monument, to tell how it was in the old days. In a sense, there is nothing personal about it; one is primarily representative of the period.

I have outlived the desire to confess my inadequacies, complain of ne-glect or mistreatment, expose the wickedness of those who run schools or armies or universities, or boast of my virtues or accomplishments. Though one recognizes as one grows older how many tricks memory plays, how often false memories screen real ones or are back-projections from family stories or unconscious desires, how hard it is to be sure what really happened and to understand either one's own motives and feelings or those of others, it is, I think, better to try to arrive at the truth than to evade or obscure the issue by deliberate fictionalizing, so that the reader is uncertain whether the author stands behind his ac-count or not. (Paul Theroux's recent quasi-fictionalized autobiography, for example, seems irritatingly evasive as compared to John Updike's straightforward attempt to be honest.[1]) It is true that the facts are not interesting or significant in themselves, but only as made so by the writer; but it is essential that the reader feel that the autobiographer respects the facts and does not play fast and loose with them.

First, inevitably, a few words about my parents. My mother grew up in Newberry and studied music at the Chicago Conservatory; when she married, she was teaching music in the Bishopville schools. She loved music, especially piano, and literature, especially poetry. Longfellow, Poe, Byron, and Kipling were favorites, all recited with exaggerated elocution and defensive self-mockery. She also took much pleasure in quoting J. Gordon Coogler, a newspaper bard who flourished, if that is the word, around the turn of the century. His most famous couplet is: "Poor South! Her books get fewer and fewer; / She was never much given to literature." (Other favorite Coogler passages deal with snow: "The snow! The snow! The beautiful snow! / The blackbird, the bluebird, and also the crow / Make tracks in the beautiful snow," and, from an elegy, "She died before the beautiful snow had melted / And was buried beneath the slush.")

My father was a self-made man. He dropped out of high school in Lamar, married, and then farmed for a few years. He quickly formed a lifelong distaste for farming, moved to Darlington and taught himself law, and became a very successful trial lawyer and prosecutor. A gifted orator and magnetic personality, he was a champion of the common man and had some affinities with the Populist movement in politics. Like most autodidacts, he was a voracious and omnivorous reader (primarily of history and current affairs, but he also shared with me a love of H. G. Wells, H. L. Mencken, *Amazing Stories,* and the *American Mercury).* Like all good trial lawyers, he was a very quick study.

With these genetic components, it was obvious that I would have to be (if not a lawyer, like my father, several of his older sons, and several of my mother's family) some combination of teacher and writer. What tipped the balance away from law was my experience of three remarkable teachers of English. Two of them were in St. John's High School

---

1. Paul Theroux, *My Secret History* (New York: Putnam's, 1989); John Updike, *Self-Consciousness: Memoirs* (New York: Knopf, 1989).

in Darlington; both were teaching in high school only because the Depression had hit in full force and interrupted their progress toward the Ph.D.s that both later completed. The first was William Stanley Hoole, who later took his Ph.D. at Duke and became a distinguished librarian, Dean of Libraries at the University of Alabama. He wrote the standard history of Charleston's Dock Street Theater and a collection of essays called *According to Hoole*.[2] His autobiographical introduction to this volume is fascinating: he was an old-fashioned humane librarian who loved books, and a colorful writer. When he left Darlington in 1931 he was succeeded by M. A. "Jake" Owings, who had an M.A. from Vanderbilt and later returned there to take his Ph.D. Owings was accustomed to teaching college students, and his English classes were far superior to what one would normally get in high school. Hoole and Owings were both attractive and impressive people, well dressed, friendly but dignified; they were good role models and made teaching seem a possible career for a boy. I was extremely lucky to have them in their few years in Darlington.

The third teacher, who was decisive for me in very many ways, was Joseph Edwards Norwood, who taught me first in my sophomore year at the University of South Carolina. (After he retired from the university, by the way, he taught for some years at the College of Charleston.) Originally from the small town of McBee, and not long back from a Rhodes Scholarship (at Oxford he had started out in law and wound up in English), he was similar to me in background, temperament, and interests, yet with what seemed to me a wealth of exotic and sophisticated experience. He loved literature and was very sensitive to it, yet he saw it as part of life, in a historical, philosophical, and moral context. Norwood took his responsibility for liberal education seriously and in the widest sense: he taught his classes not only about literature but about history, philosophy, politics, music, painting—whatever was relevant to the subject under discussion. But he had a lively sense of humor and the absurd, and was never solemn or pompous. He did little formal lecturing, preferring give-and-take dialogue with students; and

2. W. Stanley Hoole, *According to Hoole: The Collected Essays and Tales of a Scholar-Librarian and Literary Maverick* (University: University of Alabama Press, 1973).

while he never forgot his responsibilities as teacher, he treated students with respect and was genuinely interested in their ideas.

While preserving a certain distance, he was wonderfully friendly and patient with me; he willingly added to his enormous teaching load additional hours to teach honors courses for me alone, and as time went on almost adopted me as part of his family. He read my poetry and encouraged me in that direction as well as the strictly academic. With his help, and through taking courses in summer school, I was able to finish an M.A. the summer after my B.A. His life seemed nearly ideal yet possible for me, and he became my role model in earnest.

I might indulge briefly in psychological speculation at this point and note that I was the only child of my mother, who was my father's second wife, and I grew up surrounded by the numerous children of the first marriage. I was thus at once an only child and the youngest member of a large and disorderly tribe whose attitude toward me was unpredictable. I had been a premature baby, preserved by the cook in the warming oven of the wood-burning stove in the kitchen (hence inevitably called "half-baked"). Much of the time I was left with my grandmother and her stories of the Civil War and Reconstruction. My father's death when I was twelve was followed closely by the stock-market crash and the Depression. All this left me with a yearning for stability, order, tradition; some stay against the constant threat of change, deterioration, disaster. Perhaps because of this background, Norwood's specialty, eighteenth-century literature, appealed to me very strongly, and it became my specialty too through graduate school and the early part of my teaching and editing careers.

The two chief emphases that I absorbed from Norwood (though he was admirably well rounded, and interested in all aspects of literature, from the technique of verse to critical theory) were on its moral or humane significance and its relation to philosophy, or history of ideas, as represented, for instance, in Irving Babbitt's *Rousseau and Romanticism* and A. O. Lovejoy's *Great Chain of Being*. Continuing to pursue these interests through graduate school, I wrote a dissertation called *The Intellectual Background of Matthew Prior*. When I started teaching in 1940 at the University of Wisconsin, however, these interests were obliged to take a back seat: the currently dominant concern was with the uses of language, and what seemed most urgent was to teach the students to discriminate between these uses—or, to put it crudely, how to detect propaganda and manipulation, either in political speeches or in advertisements. These were, of course, developments of the trend exemplified by I. A. Richards and C. K. Ogden's *Meaning of Meaning;* but at Wisconsin a textbook by S. I. Hayakawa (later famous as a U.S. Senator) called *Language in Action* was used, and there was much talk of Korzybski's Abstraction Ladder and other slightly flaky extensions. But it was a very tolerant and lively environment, and those who preferred "traditional" approaches, as I did, were allowed to use them unmolested.

After four years in the military, when I lost touch almost completely with the academic scene, but was thus confirmed in my belief that that scene was the one I wanted to inhabit for the rest of my life, I returned to teaching at Vanderbilt in 1946. At Vanderbilt I encountered the Fugitive-Agrarian tradition, still very much alive there, and gradually met its writers. I sat in on Donald Davidson's classes and met Warren and Tate and the others. I reviewed Tate's poetry for a Nashville newspaper, some of his friends sent him the review, and he wrote me a note of thanks. When his next critical book appeared, he suggested to John Palmer, editor of the *Sewanee Review,* that he have me review it. Both Tate and Palmer were pleased with the review, and so began my friendships with both men and my writing for the magazine that led to my becoming editor a few years later. Oddly enough, I first met Palmer in London rather than Tennessee; we proved congenial, and he invited me to lecture at Sewanee and then arranged for me to spend a summer there; so when the editorship became open I already knew and was known by the Sewanee community. Another fortuitous but fortunate circumstance.

In teaching, it was an extremely challenging and exciting time: many of the students were veterans, older and more experienced than the norm, and at Vanderbilt some (for example, James Dickey and Madison Jones) were highly gifted writers. Everyone was committed to making up for lost time: the imperatives were to make sure that students learned to read and write properly as fast as possible, and the chief instrument was the so-called New Criticism, as embodied in the Brooks and

Warren textbooks and their imitators. After some initial resistance—my graduate school training had been entirely historical, though humane— I became a pragmatic convert, while still practicing historical research and other kinds of interpretation. I finished and published my historical research on the ethical, religious, and scientific contexts of Prior's works, and I began, in collaboration with another scholar, the enormous task of editing all Prior's writings.

At Sewanee, the chief problem was how to find time to fulfill all my obligations simultaneously: editing the *Sewanee Review* with little assistance (in itself a more than full-time job), continuing work on the Prior edition, teaching half-time, and trying to get some critical writing of my own done. One of the most rewarding aspects of Sewanee life was the friendship of remarkable fellow teachers like Charles Harrison and Andrew Lytle; another was the experience of teaching the small but never-failing succession of exceptionally talented students (two of whom, Bernie Dunlap and Richard Tillinghast, are here tonight). At Sewanee, the smaller and more intimate setting encouraged closer relations with students than was customary at Vanderbilt.

From teaching I learned much about myself as well as much about the nature of the exercise and some of its forms. (There are, of course, very many different kinds of teaching and as many different kinds of good teachers as there are different kinds of students; the notion that one size fits all is pure illusion, though widespread.) For myself, teaching was intimately related to research and writing, rather than opposed to or competing with them; since I found repetition boring, I preferred discussion with small groups to formal lectures, because this format allowed for stimulating interaction and for spontaneity on both sides. Coeducation always seemed to me more attractive than unisex, because girls tend to be more complaisant and docile than boys and provide a nice counterpoint to masculine audacity and competitiveness, and the repressed sexual awareness tends to be stimulating to everyone.

Teaching is an impossible profession, in the same sense as psychiatry and especially psychoanalysis: nobody is ever well enough qualified, nobody can do it as well as it should be done, and its results, beyond a basic minimum, are almost wholly unpredictable. The good teacher, like the good psychoanalyst, strives to make himself unnecessary; if he succeeds, the student is independent and no longer needs him. But the future development of the student, and hence the impact of the teaching on him, is unpredictable. For me, the important thing was the effect I seemed to be having on a limited number of students, not reaching large numbers. But the effect is a "transference," just as in psychoanalysis, an artificially close relationship, and it is as important for the teacher as for the analyst not to mistake it for a normal relationship and thus neither to abuse nor overvalue it. Teaching has its dangers of ego inflation (since many students tend to flatter) and despair, when it seems unnecessary for good students and useless for bad; it was always, for me, at once frustrating and rewarding.

Editing an eighteenth-century text taught me how precarious and uncertain the physical existence of a text is, as well as how hard it is to get back to the writer's final intention (in, for example, *Piers Plowman,* many of Shakespeare's plays, Joyce's *Ulysses).* One may, of course, approach this problem from the other, or writer's, end: as Auden says (quoting Valéry), a poem is never finished, only abandoned, and only after the author is dead can one posit a truly final state of any work. In some cases it is clear that the author never made up his mind which version he considered final. The survival of past texts is haphazard: consider how much of classical literature was lost in the great fire of the library at Alexandria alone, and how much valuable material may still remain in dark corners of closets and trunks in Britain and this country. Attempting to recover and provide in notes and commentary for the reader the context of a text some three centuries old made me keenly aware of the impossibility of doing so adequately.

Unfortunately for me, textual editing overlapped in my case with a very different kind, the editing of a literary quarterly. Editing this kind of magazine made me very conscious of the split between the minority or elite audience and the mass audience, and of how much money is involved in literature considered as a commercial artifact and how little in literature considered as art. The so-called little magazines would love to be big and appeal to a much larger audience; they will do almost anything to do so except compromise their standards; but the audience for serious criticism, fiction, and poetry remains preposterously small and mostly academic. As Randall Jarrell memorably said, the happy few grow fewer and unhappier all the time, while the population increases by leaps and bounds. There are, of course, fortunate exceptions: fiction, especially when made into successful movies, has made some good writers rich; and even some poets have prospered, though usually more from lecturing, reading, and hackwork than from poetry proper. Being the coexecutor of W. H. Auden's estate gave me an inside view of the financial side of the literary life.

I published my first poem when I was twelve, and have still not completely extinguished the hope of writing a really good one tomorrow. But I came to the conclusion early in college that my talent was a minor one, and that poetry would have to be an avocation while my career was based on teaching and criticism. This was certainly a sensible decision; was it possibly too sensible? Maybe, but I still don't think that renouncing everything else and starving in a garret like Chatterton would have increased my chances of becoming a great poet. I have published enough to prove to myself that I can write genuine poetry, that it is not alien or forbidden territory; and I think this has been essential to my performance as critic. (Are there any good critics who have not written at least a little good poetry or fiction? I doubt it.)

As critic, I have seen my work as mostly an extension of the teaching function: I have attempted to make sense of contemporary writers and of the literary scene, writing with the intelligent common reader in mind. I have not been interested in "power," political correctness, or critical theory in the contemporary sense. I have never believed criticism should be autonomous; I think it should try to be useful to readers and even to writers. I don't believe literature is dead or dying or that the future lies in television or multimedia. My aim has been to integrate, against the strong centrifugal and separatist pressures of our times, the creative and the critical, the study of language, philosophy, and history in the broadest sense, in the study of literature. This was my aim as magazine editor and as teacher, and is still my aim as critic.

My criticism has never been exclusively literary, but also cultural in the sense that I have seen literature in historical, moral, and philosophical contexts. I renounced aestheticism and escapism when I went to college and repented of my earlier enthusiasm for Swinburne and James Branch Cabell. Since that time I have tried to be a responsible interpreter

of literature in its cultural, moral, and intellectual context, not detached
in any aesthetic otherworld. On the other hand, I haven't taken part in
the arguments about political correctness and the curriculum that make
up the "culture wars," or multicultural criticism in what has come to
be a specialized contemporary sense.

In my *Poetry of W. H. Auden: The Disenchanted Island,*[3] I was interested
in Auden's relation to the whole earlier history of English and American
literature, and so my point of view was historical in this sense; but I was
drawn to him first because of the relevance of his ideas to contemporary
dilemmas in philosophy, religion, and science, as well as by his technical
virtuosity and his skill as satirist and comic writer. These are exactly
the same interests that drew me to Matthew Prior and my long task of
interpreting and editing his work in terms primarily historical. While
I hope all this work was illuminated by the "New Criticism," it was at
the opposite pole from what is sometimes thought of as typical New
Criticism focused on the text alone.

My *Dionysus and the City: Modernism in Twentieth-Century Poetry*[4]
was an attempt to do the same kind of thing for the whole modern
movement in English and American verse, placing it in the context
of the history of the other arts and modern culture generally from
Nietzsche on. I count myself lucky to have found poets so congenial
as Prior and Auden to work on, and to have known Auden in the last
decade of his life, as well as many of the others discussed in the *Dionysus*
book, especially Allen Tate, Robert Penn Warren, and James Dickey.
The two books of selected essays I have published since my retirement,
American Ambitions[5] and *Countries of the Mind,*[6] have employed the same
approach in discussing a wide variety of writers.

But after such a high-sounding statement of intentions and motives
I feel that it might be more honest to say, as a candid friend did in the

---

3. (New York: Oxford University Press, 1963; rev. paperback ed., 1968).

4. (New York: Oxford University Press, 1970).

5. *American Ambitions: Selected Essays on Literary and Cultural Themes* (Baltimore:
Johns Hopkins University Press, 1987).

6. *Countries of the Mind: Literary Explorations* (Columbia: University of Missouri Press,
1992).

army, that what I have always really liked best to do is just sit around and read.

To return to the beginning, I believe that writers should avoid autobiography: it's a mug's game at which you can't win and a waste of resources. But when you reach a certain age, and feel yourself becoming a part of history, the impulse to sum up your part before someone else does it for you becomes very strong; and I hope you will forgive me if, warmed by the euphoria of the present delightful occasion, I have indulged in this brief retrospect of my world as I see it tonight.

INDEX